The Big Book of
100
Outdoor
Activities

The Big Book of
100
Outdoor
Activities

Laura Minter
& Tia Williams

First published 2018 by
Guild of Master Craftsman Publications Ltd
Castle Place, 166 High Street, Lewes,
East Sussex, BN7 1XU, UK

ISBN 978 1 78494 404 9

Publisher Jonathan Bailey
Production Manager Jim Bulley
Senior Project Editor Sara Harper
Editor Sarah Doughty
Managing Art Editor Gilda Pacitti
Art Editor Luana Gobbo
Photography Laura Minter and Tia Williams
Picture credit Page 11: Shutterstock/Wavebreakmedia
Illustrator Mia Underwood

Set in Cabin and Riffic
Colour origination by GMC Reprographics
Printed and bound in Turkey

A note on measurements
The imperial measurements in these projects are converted from
metric. While every attempt has been made to ensure that they
are as accurate as possible, some rounding up or down has been
inevitable. For this reason, it is always best to stick to one system or
the other throughout a project: do not mix metric and imperial units.

Contents

Games

Rainy day

Food and drink

Playing and make-believe

Introduction

In this book you will find 100 quick and simple projects designed to get kids outdoors and enjoying nature. The pages are filled with a range of things to do outside, including crafts using natural objects, activities to encourage wildlife to your garden and toys and games for outdoor play. There are imaginative ideas for creative activities on rainy days and also some simple recipes for kids to follow, either using ingredients you can find in the garden, food you can cook outdoors, or bakes inspired by nature.

We have divided the book into sections to enable you to dip in and out depending on what you would like to do, what kind of mood your child is in or what kind of mood the weather is in!

We believe that developing a child's interest in nature, wildlife and the outdoors is one of the most important things you can do. They may need a little nudge to go out on a walk but there are so many fascinating things to see and do that it doesn't take much to get them interested and engaged with their environment. And this can be on any scale – out in the woods, in the garden or even just watching a sunflower seed grow in a pot on the windowsill. Teaching children about their environment encourages them to explore and be more curious about their world and to care more deeply about it.

We've wanted to write a nature-inspired craft book ever since we wrote *The Big Book of 100 Little Activities*. We love being outdoors and making things using natural objects, and so do our children. Every time we go out our kids come home with pocketfuls of leaves, acorns, pebbles and armfuls of sticks. For a while these things piled up by the back door, but then we started putting them to good use. We realized just how many cool things you can make from things found in nature, and how much our children enjoyed making them. More importantly, they love these home-made personal things just as much as the mountains of plastic toys we've accumulated over the years.

We each have two restless children obsessed with crafting (like their mums). All the projects in this book have been designed with them (and children like them) in mind. Our kids have dutifully helped create each and every one and when a project didn't work, they were only too happy to tell us. You'll be pleased to know those ones didn't make the cut! The 100 projects featured in this book all have the seal of approval from our Little Buttons. Happy crafting!

Getting started

Here is a quick overview of some of the craft materials you'll find useful for the activities in this book. Our biggest tip for all of the projects, however, is to not simply go out and buy the materials suggested, but to try and use what you already have and adapt the makes according to that – and what your child wants to do. It will result in a more personal craft that kids will probably love more.

Having said that, a crate full of craft goodies for your children to dip into is, in our books, a pretty great thing to have. It will encourage independent play (which means a cup of tea for you) and boost their imaginations. Just make sure you keep the glitter on a high shelf well out of reach...

Nature materials

Crafting using things sourced from nature is great as it's always twofold – you get to have fun sticking all your bits and pieces together but you also get to go on a treasure hunt to collect them first. Be prepared by always having a carrier bag with you when out to collect your supplies.

Here are some of the natural materials we use most frequently in the book, so you can build up a bit of a stash if you want to:

• Leaves
• Twigs
• Pine cones
• Feathers
• Pebbles and shells

Things you'll need

PAINT, BRUSHES AND SPONGES The projects in this book use child-friendly, washable paint unless otherwise stated. Having a range of brushes in different sizes is great, as well as sponges, combs and other things that allow children to play with the texture of paint.

GLUE Where possible we try to use PVA and glue sticks for the projects, but with natural materials it can help to have something a little stronger to encourage longevity. Keep some superglue on hand, and a glue gun if you have one (obviously for adult use only!)

TAPE Double-sided tape is our favourite item for kiddie crafting! Mess free and with an instant stick, it's a total winner. Masking tape, sticky tape and decorative tapes are also used in this book.

PAPER AND CARD A mixed pack of coloured paper and card and a set of paper plates, cups and tubes give you a great base for making lots of different things.

EMBELLISHMENTS Googly eyes, buttons, beads, sequins, ribbons, pipe cleaners and lollipop sticks make crafting a bit more interesting for kids and add a great final touch to any project.

RECYCLED ITEMS Raid the recycling box for cardboard tubes, boxes, containers and jars as they can be turned into all sorts of wonderful things. Keep them all together in a box if you have the room, so that you can rummage through to make something whenever you feel like it.

Safety

It's really important when crafting with younger kids to make sure they are properly supervised with equipment. The projects in this book are intended for children with adult assistance. Items such as drills, craft knives, secateurs, sharp scissors, and strong glue must of course only be used by an adult. Other materials and processes that should be done by an adult are stated, where applicable, in the projects.

Tips for crafting with kids

TAKE A CARRIER BAG When you're out and about, carry a bag with you so that if you spot something that would be good for crafting, you can collect it up easily, without having to fill your pockets.

DO A CRAFT PROJECT OUTSIDE An alternative to taking materials home to craft is to do the craft in an outdoor place and leave it for others to admire (the land art on page 82 is a good example). Take a photograph of your finished masterpiece to take home instead.

KEEP AN OLD SET OF CLOTHES It is worth keeping old clothes on hand for outdoor adventures so you don't have to worry about mud and mess. It's a good idea to keep these in your car with a pair of wellies, so that you can change in and out of them when you need to.

LET KIDS LEAD THE CRAFTING The activities should be seen as a starting point, not to be taken prescriptively. If kids want to turn sticks into a wand, broom or anything else let them go with it – they'll enjoy it more.

BE ORGANIZED AND PREPARED This is essential for any type of crafting with young children. Have your materials sorted in little pots and laid out ready to go. You'll all find it much more enjoyable if you aren't darting off to find tape halfway through.

GET OUT IN ALL SEASONS Outdoor play isn't only for sunny days. As long as you take appropriate clothing you can get out in all weather. Forests in the rain are particularly magical, and kids love being outside getting wet – as long as you have something dry and snuggly to change into.

MAKE KIDS PROUD OF THEIR WORK You can do this by displaying your kids' art. But if you don't want to keep ALL the pieces they make you can always take photos of them and put the photos into an album.

Wildlife spotting

1 Twig bird box

You'll need quite a few twigs for this project, so head out to the woods with the children and take a sack to put the collected twigs in. You will need to do this project in different sessions to allow time for the glue to dry. Balsa wood is fantastic for crafting with kids as it is soft enough to cut with scissors or a craft knife.

You will need
Sack (for collection)
A pile of dry, straight twigs, about ½in (1cm) thick
Secateurs
Wood glue
2 sheets of 2mm thick balsa wood, about 6 x 6in
    (15 x 15cm) in size
Craft knife

1 Make a panel of twigs for the base of the box. An adult should cut 12–15 twigs into 6in (15cm) lengths using secateurs. Glue the twigs together on a flat surface. Glue two more twigs across the others on the bottom for added strength.

2 To make the front of the bird box, measure the width of the base, excluding the outer two twigs. Draw a line on the balsa wood to this measurement and add a domed shape around it, 5–6in (12–15cm) high. Cut out carefully, using a craft knife, then cut a 1½in (4cm) square from the centre along the bottom. Use this as a template to create one more dome, without the central hole.

3 Glue each dome onto the ends of the bird box, between the two outer twigs. Leave to dry – you might need to prop the wood against a firm surface to keep it upright at this point.

4 Cut more 6in (15cm) long twigs – you'll need around 25–30 of these. Glue them onto the bird box, around the two wooden domes.

5 All you need to do now is to find a suitable sturdy spot for your bird box, either wedged gently in place on a tree or nailed onto a branch.

Nature spotter game

This simple game encourages children to look for and learn about wildlife. You can take it with you on a walk and see how many different things you can cross off. Use the pictures here as a guideline for what to include, but try to tailor it to what you are likely to find in your local area. Children can draw or colour in their own pictures, using books and the internet for help if needed.

You will need
Black pen and ruler
1 sheet of A5 card per person
Pencil
Felt-tip pens
Sticky-back plastic
Board markers

1 At home, use a black pen and ruler to draw a rectangle in the centre of the card, measuring 5 x 7in (12 x 18cm). Divide this up into 1in (3cm) squares to create a grid.

2 Fill in columns 1 and 3 (leaving empty squares next to each picture) with birds, insects, plants, trees and other things you might see in your local area. Draw in pencil then colour in with felt-tip pens.

3 Cover the front and back of the card with sticky-back plastic. Now you're ready to play while you are out and about. Use a board marker to tick off all the things you find, then wipe your card clean at the end.

Because the game is covered in plastic, it can be played over and over again!

3

DIY terrarium

If kept properly, a snail can live for up to 15 years. That's quite a commitment!

This mini world is easy to make and looks really nice on a shelf. If your child wants to, the terrarium can be turned into a home for a small snail - see the last step for details. With a little care, snails can make fantastic pets for children!

1 Make sure the inside of the jar is completely dry, then pour a layer of sand into the bottom. Add a layer of gravel and a layer of soil. Pat down with a spoon.

2 Go outside and find anything that would be nice for your terrarium – moss is perfect, but also small clumps of clover, sedum or anything else that grows easily. You will need to dig them up with the roots and soil attached using a small trowel. Add to your jar and press down. Add a little soil around the roots.

3 Finally, add a nice twig to your terrarium and a drop of water.

4 At this point, if you like you can add a small snail to keep as a pet. If you do this, punch small holes in the lid for air, keep it in a cool place, spritz with water every other day to keep moist and remember to give your snail food – strawberries, lettuce, cucumber and egg shells are favourites. A snail needs calcium to strengthen its shell, so add a little chalk or cuttlefish bone to the jar (egg shell has calcium too).

You will need
Large glass jam jar, cleaned with labels removed
Sand, gravel and soil, about 2 tbsp of each
Spoon
Clumps of moss, clover or sedum
Small trowel
Small twig
Drop of water
Snail and snail food (optional)

Bird's nest

4

This is a great way to teach children about how birds make their nests. Encourage children to pretend to be a bird, hunting for nest-building materials then weaving a nest with only the things that they find. Try to do this activity in spring when birds will be building their nests too. You can pop your nest into a tree and it might even find an owner!

You will need
Twigs, vines, feathers, moss
and long grass
Bucket for collecting
String (optional)

1 Begin by collecting any materials in a bucket that would be good for a nest. Have a chat about what would be good for the frame of the nest, what would be good for weaving the shape, and what would make soft padding for baby birds. Strong, bendy grasses and vines are good for creating the initial shape.

2 Start the nest by creating a small hoop from vines and grasses. Twist and tie strands together until you have a sturdy base. This can be tricky for small children – if they're struggling, you can cheat a little and tie together with string.

3 Make the base of the nest by twisting vines onto the sides and looping underneath to the other side. Do this three or four times until it feels quite sturdy. (Again, if it's a struggle, get the string out!)

4 Now you can build up the structure of the nest by weaving small twigs, dried leaves and grass into the framework. Once most of the nest is covered you can add softer materials like feathers, old bits of string, wool and moss to the nest. Poke them in with a stick – mimicking a bird's beak – and your nest is finished.

5 Pop your nest in a tree between branches and see if any birds show interest. They might just use the materials you collected to start building their own nest!

Miniature pond

5

This is a lovely way to get children interested in pond life on a miniature scale, and a great way to encourage frogs, toads and newts into your garden. You can buy pond plants inexpensively from your local garden centre. You will need a large waterproof container, such as an old sink, sturdy bucket or washing-up bowl.

You will need
A large waterproof container
Pebbles and gravel
Rainwater
Large rocks, bricks or
    roof tiles
1 or 2 pond plants

Position your pond container in a shady spot. Add some gravel to the bottom, then fill it up with water (rainwater is best). Add a couple of large rocks along the wall inside and outside the container so that the wildlife can easily get into the pond. Add your pond plants and place another rock or roof tile securely over one side of the pond to give a little shade and make a hiding place for creatures. Check back on your pond in a few weeks to see if any animals have appeared!

6 Pine-cone bird feeder

Going on a hunt for pine cones is part of the fun with this project, but don't despair if you can't find any! You can always buy them in garden centres or online – just make sure you pick unscented ones.

Tie the string around the stems. Spread peanut butter all over the pine cones with a knife – get in between the bristles and ensure the whole cone is covered. Pour some birdseed onto a plate and roll the cones in the seed and pour it into the gaps. Then hang the three pine cones together in a tree, sit back and wait for the birdies to flock for their breakfast. Once all the seeds are gone you can repeat the process and refill the cones.

You will need
Smooth peanut butter
Knife (for spreading)
3 pine cones
Birdseed
Plate
String

Bug hotel

7

Bugs need a nice place to rest their heads, and this simple construction will create a lovely home for lots of critters in your garden. Have a look around and see what you can find that would make a good addition to the hotel – you aren't restricted by what is listed here. Instead of the bricks, for example, you could use old wooden pallets, and terracotta pots make good homes for frogs and toads.

You will need
About 12 bricks
Thin piece of plywood (about 18 x 18in/ 50 x 50cm)
Old roof tiles
Sticks, bamboo, straw, corrugated card, pine cones, pebbles and leaves
Chalk

1 Make the structure of the bug hotel. Find a flat, sheltered area in your garden and clear any debris away. Lay out three rows of bricks, two layers high. Put the plywood on the top of this and adjust the bricks so that they fit the length of the wood. Add another row of bricks, then put some tiles on the top for the roof.

2 Fill each 'room' in your hotel with things the bugs will like. Use bamboo canes for bees, which like to nest in the little holes. Ladybirds and other beetles like sticks, dry leaves and straw. Centipedes and spiders like bits of bark, frogs like large pebbles and lacewings like corrugated card.

3 Finally, give your hotel a name and write it in chalk on a piece of roof tile. Prop onto the top of the hotel with the help of a rock, and your hotel is officially open for bees-ness (tee hee!)

8

Woodland walks

Woodlands are filled with loads of great things to engage children with wildlife, but it can sometimes be impossible to get them interested in going for a walk. Here are our 10 top tips to encourage them to head off into the woods, whatever the weather.

1 Bring a bucket – to collect things from the woods to turn into a collage when you get home.

2 Take a magnifying glass – to inspect all the creepy crawlies you find on your way.

3 Make yourself a nature spotter game (see page 17) – and tick off all the things you find.

4 Bring a change of clothes – so that you're less worried about messy or wet clothes. That way you can jump in puddles and not care!

5 Take crayons and paper with you – to make bark and leaf rubbings.

6 Take photographs – if children have their own cameras they can practise using them. If not, let them help you.

7 Hunt for footprints – see if you can identify them and follow them to find out where they go.

8 Go on a nature treasure hunt – to search for pine cones, moss, conkers or acorns. The first to find the treasure wins a point.

9 Take a jar – to act as a pond viewer. See what you can see under the surface of ponds and puddles – being careful not to fall in!

10 Do a coin walk – take a coin out with you and every time you reach a fork in the path flip a coin to decide which way to go.

In the garden

9

Milk-bottle watering can

This simple upcycling project transforms an empty plastic milk bottle into a watering can. Make a whole bunch of them with different-sized bottles, then decorate to personalize!

You will need
Plastic milk bottle
Masking tape
Acrylic paint
PVA glue
Paintbrush
Screwdriver (or metal skewer)
Water

1 Remove any labels from the bottle and give it a wash inside and out. Put the lid to one side. Use masking tape to mark out a funky design on the bottle.

2 Mix acrylic paint with PVA in equal quantities, to make a paint that will easily stick to the plastic bottle. Paint the bottle and leave it to dry.

3 Carefully peel off the masking tape to reveal your design.

4 Use a small screwdriver or skewer to pierce small holes in the bottle lid. Adults should, of course, do this part.

5 Fill the bottle with water and screw the lid on. Now you can water the garden!

Newspaper seedling pots

Make your own biodegradable pots to plant seeds in, which can then be transferred outside into pots or the ground when the seeds start to sprout. The newspaper will biodegrade into the soil, making it a great way to transfer seedlings without damaging them.

You will need
Sheets of newspaper (1 sheet makes 3 pots)
Empty jam jar
Trowel
Soil (or compost)
Packet of flower or vegetable seeds
Tray
Water

1 Cut the newspaper into 5in (13cm) wide strips from the length of the paper. Place the jar at one end of the newspaper strip so half the paper is over the bottom of the jar. Wrap the paper around the jar.

2 To make the bottom of your pot, fold the excess newspaper into the middle on the bottom of the jar, folding a little bit at a time working your way around the jar. Slide the jar out.

3 Pop the pots on a tray, fill them halfway with soil and drop the seeds in. Leave the seedling pots in a sunny spot for a few days, watering them regularly.

4 When the seeds start to sprout, use a trowel to dig a hole in the flowerbed, push the pot in and press the soil around it.

11 Grassy caterpillars

These cute caterpillars take a little time to get hairy, so mini gardeners will need to wait for the finished result. Making and looking after them is all part of the garden fun!

You will need
Soil (or compost)
Tray
Grass seed
Scissors
Pairs of nude tights
    (20 denier or less)
String
Coloured pipe cleaners
Strong glue
Pair of googly eyes

1 Tip the soil into a tray and sprinkle a generous amount (about 15 tablespoons) of grass seed into it. Mix the seeds into the soil.

2 Cut the legs off a pair of tights and fill one with the soil and seed mixture. Fill it to the length you would like your caterpillar to be and tie a knot in it. A rough guideline would be an adult handful for each section of the caterpillar. You want the caterpillar to be nice and plump!

3 Tie pieces of string onto the tights to create the sections of the caterpillar. Cut off any remainder of the tights.

4 Wrap a pipe cleaner around the string sections and bend the ends to resemble legs. Cut another pipe cleaner into quarters and glue two antennae onto the front of the caterpillar, along with some googly eyes.

5 Make the other caterpillar from the second leg of the tights. Watch them both grow into hairy creatures – the grass will take a couple of days to sprout but leave it longer to get nice bushy caterpillars. Once the grass has grown, give them a little haircut so they can see!

Try growing different-shaped creatures, such as hedgehogs, butterflies or even people!

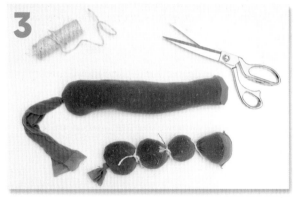

12

Plant-pot birdbath

This easy birdbath is made from terracotta pots that can be decorated by children in any design they like. We've used finger printing to create the flowers, but hand or foot printing would work just as well. Remember to supervise kids when using acrylic paint as it will stain clothes and surfaces!

You will need
3 terracotta pots, about
    5in (13cm) high
1 terracotta dish, about
    9in (24cm) diameter
Strong adhesive
Acrylic paint
Craft varnish and
    paintbrush
Water

1 Glue two terracotta pots together at their bases. Add glue around one of the rims and attach the third pot, rim to rim on top. Once the glue has set on the pots, glue the dish on top of the top pot in the middle.

2 Paint the whole birdbath with acrylic paint, using several layers to get an even coverage.

3 To make the flowers, dip little fingers into paint and thumbprint the flower petals on. Clean the children's hands well afterwards.

4 Add a coat of varnish to protect the pot from the weather. Fill with water and put in the garden.

Shadow drawing

13

This is a very simple sunny-day activity that will keep kids busy in the park or garden. The longest shadows will be cast early in the morning or late in the afternoon.

When the sun is out, roll the paper out and set it up in a place where a shadow is being cast. Kids can then draw the shadows of the trees, flowers or people onto paper to create a cool picture they can colour in later with felt-tip pens or paint.

You will need
Roll of paper
Pencils
Felt-tip pens
Child-friendly paints
Paintbrushes

14 Garden pinwheel

Pick colourful, contrasting card, preferably with a pattern on it, to make your pinwheel. We used a dowel for the stem, but you could also use a pencil with an eraser, pushing the pin into the eraser part. This pinwheel is made from paper, so it won't survive a downpour. If you want it to be more permanent, try using thin sheets of plastic or craft foam.

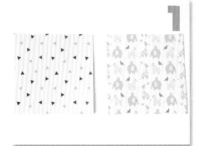

You will need
Pencil and ruler
Scissors
2 pieces of matching coloured card (or plastic sheets or craft foam)
Glue stick
Eraser
Drawing pin
Dowel (or pencil with eraser)

1 Cut out two 4in (10cm) squares from different coloured pieces of card. Glue them back to back, making sure you glue the whole square, and leave to dry.

2 Draw a line from one corner of the card to the other, then repeat for the other corner. Make a mark 2in (5cm) up each line, and cut up to this point. Rub the pencil lines out with the eraser.

3 Pull the left-hand side of each corner into the centre, bending them gently in. Poke a drawing pin through the end of each one, then push the pin through the centre of the paper.

4 If you are using a dowel, soak it in water first to soften the wood. Push the pin into the end of the dowel or pencil eraser. Give the pinwheel a good wiggle to make it loose, then pop in the garden for a nice touch of colour.

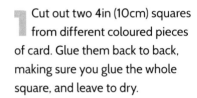

Mini fruit and veg patch

15

You don't need a garden to have a vegetable patch – this mini one can go on a balcony or window ledge in a sunny spot and will allow kids to produce their favourite foods. Acrylic paint is best for this project as it is weatherproof, so remember to cover clothes and surfaces.

You will need
Wooden crate, about 16 x 6in
   (40 x 15cm)
Acrylic paint in a range
   of colours
Paintbrushes
Soil (or compost)
Fruit and vegetable seeds

1 Personalize your vegetable crate by painting it however you like, using acrylic paint.

2 Leave to dry, then fill with soil. Select your seeds and plant them, following the instructions on the packet. Choose plants that are easy to grow and don't get too large. Strawberries, carrots, beetroot, spring onions and tomatoes would all grow well with a little TLC. Place in a warm and sunny spot, watering regularly, and watch your seedlings grow into delicious fruit or vegetables.

16 Flowerpot person

This cute little flowerpot lady makes a nice addition to your garden or windowsill.
You can fill her with soil and seeds, or a plant, to give her a lovely head of hair.

You will need

Scissors
Ball of string
Strong glue
1 flowerpot, about 5in (13cm) high
1 flowerpot, about 4in (10cm) high

2 mini flowerpots, about 2in (5cm) high
Acrylic paint
Paintbrushes
Handful of colourful beads
Soil (or compost)
Herbs or flowers

1 Cut a 10in (25cm) length of string and glue it centrally onto the bottom of the largest flowerpot to create the arms. Glue the medium-sized flowerpot on top of the larger pot. Cut two pieces of string 6in (15cm) long for the legs and glue onto the inside of the larger flowerpot.

2 Use acrylic paint to add a face to the top flowerpot, and a collar and buttons to the bottom flowerpot.

3 Thread beads onto the arms, finishing with a large bead at each end, and tie a double knot at the bottom to secure. Thread beads onto the legs and the small flowerpots onto the ends. Tie the leg strings with knots and secure with glue.

4 Fill the top flowerpot with soil, then add your favourite herbs or flowers for hair.

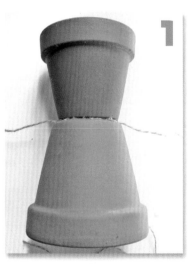

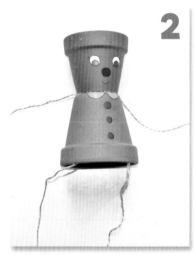

Recycled planters

17

Why throw away old bits and bobs when they can be given a new lease of life in the garden? Keep old wellies, toys, pots and cups to make unique garden planters.

Simply use your old toys or wellies as containers for plants. To help the water drain easily, make some holes in the bottom using a drill or sharp knife. Place a few rocks in the bottom before filling with soil and then adding your plants or seeds.

You will need
Old toys or old wellies
  (or old pots or cups)
Drill or sharp knife
Rocks
Soil (or compost)
Plants or seeds

18 Lollipop bird feeder

This bird feeder is made only from lollipop sticks and it's really easy to build. It looks attractive hanging in the garden and birds will flock to the feeder if you fill it with their favourite snacks.

You will need
About 75 wooden
   lollipop sticks
Wood glue
String
Bird food

For a quicker make, you could create a triangular or square-shaped lollipop feeder.

1 Glue five lollipop sticks together to make a pentagon shape (you will need to overlap them at the ends).

2 Arrange and glue more sticks over the top to create a base. It doesn't really matter how you do this, so long as there are no gaps.

3 Glue another five lollipop sticks around the edge, again to make a pentagon. Repeat eight to ten times to create the sides of the feeder.

4 Tie a length of string onto each side of the feeder – each length should be about 10in (25cm), with one being about 20in (50cm). Tie together 8in (20cm) along each length so that it hangs evenly.

5 Hang the feeder in a tree and fill with birdseed, bread or mealworms.

1

2

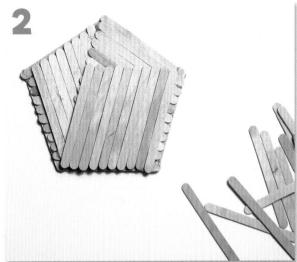

3

4

5

19 Personalized tin pots

Old tin cans are great for garden activities, such as the tin-can bowling game on page 90 or for making sweet little plant pots like these, which encourage children to show an interest in growing and caring for flowers and herbs. The pots can be painted in two ways – either with chalkboard paint so that children can label their plants or personalized with acrylics.

You will need
Black chalkboard paint
Selection of old tin cans, cleaned with
    labels removed
Chalk
Acrylic paint in a variety of colours
Paintbrushes

1 Paint a base coat of black chalkboard paint onto the cans. Label them in white chalk with whichever plants you are growing. Herbs and sunflowers make great first plants for children.

2 Alternatively, you can decorate and personalize pots by painting a pattern or coloured picture onto the cans using acrylic paints.

Be sure to cover clothing and surfaces when letting kids use acrylics.

Paper-plate sundial

This is a great project to introduce children to time telling, and show how our clocks relate to the position of the Sun. It's really quick to make with a few basic craft supplies.

You will need
Paper plate
Ruler
Sticky putty
Pencil or pen
Coloured pens

You will need to do this on a sunny day when shadows are cast on the ground.

1 Divide the back of the plate into 12 equal sections. The easiest way to do this is mark each quarter point first with a ruler, then add two points between each quarter. Mark each point in pen and add a colourful number to resemble a clock.

2 Find and mark the centre of the plate using a ruler. Place a piece of sticky putty on the other side and push the sharp end of a pencil or pen through the point. This will make the stick part (which is called the gnomon) of the sundial. Make sure it is pointing up straight. Now simply place the sundial in a sunny spot in the garden, so that a shadow is cast onto it. Look at the time and turn the dial so that it points at the correct number. Mark where the shadow falls in pencil. Leave it for an hour or so, then return and see where your sundial points to now. You can keep marking the points to keep a record of the time.

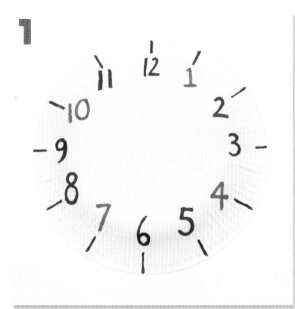

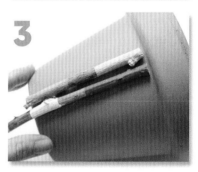

21

Painted twig pot

Jazz up a terracotta flowerpot with twigs and a lick of paint. Go on a twig hunt and get painting!

You will need
Twigs
Masking tape
Acrylic paints
Paintbrushes
Pencil
Terracotta flowerpot
Secateurs
Strong glue

1 Snap the twigs roughly to the same length as the pot from the rim to the base. Add masking tape to sections of twigs, spacing the tape out randomly.

2 Paint the twigs with several coats of paint in different colours and leave to dry.

3 Remove the tape and start arranging the twigs onto the pot. Place them under the rim, mark where the twigs hits the bottom of the pot and snip off the remainder using secateurs.

4 Glue the twigs onto the pot all the way around.

Garden sprinkler

22

This sprinkler reuses a bottle from your recycling box and helps you to cool you down on a hot sunny day! It sprays water in every direction, providing endless fun jumping through and dodging the water, as well as giving your grass a drink. If you don't have a drill you could use a pair of scissors or a screwdriver to poke the holes in the bottle.

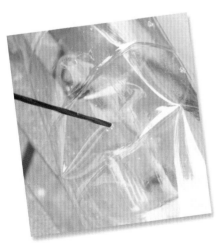

You will need
2-litre plastic bottle
Drill with 4mm drill bit
   (optional) or screwdriver
Hose attached to tap
Duct tape

Remove the lid and label from the bottle and give it a good clean. Lay the bottle on its side and make two lines of holes using a drill, if available (otherwise a screwdriver works well). You will need about ten holes spread out over the length of the bottle. Pop the hose into the top of the bottle and seal it in place with duct tape. Stand back, turn the tap on and prepare to get wet!

Messy
makes

26 Water wall

This is a really fun summer activity that uses piping, funnels and bottles to catch rainwater. Use a large piece of pegboard so the water wall can be stored away – or you could keep it all year, attached to an outside wall. Look for the materials to use in your shed, but also have a dig around for old vacuum-cleaner pipes, plastic bottles and sieves.

You will need

Piece of pegboard, at least
   3ft (1m) square in size
2 plastic milk bottles
Funnels
3 pieces of flexible pipe,
   about 3ft (1m) long
Plastic tubes
Screwdriver (or metal skewer)
Cable ties
Dish

1 Lay the pegboard flat and arrange the bottles and funnels into two or three rows on the board, working down from the top. Cut the bottom off two milk bottles and remove the lids. Start with the cut-open milk bottles and funnels at the top of the board and think about how the water will flow through when arranging the pipes and tubes. The pieces should all meet in the middle at the bottom.

2 Poke holes into one side using a screwdriver, near the bottom of each milk bottle (an adult should, of course, do this part). Use cable ties to attach the bottles onto the top of the board.

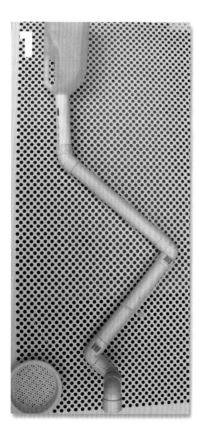

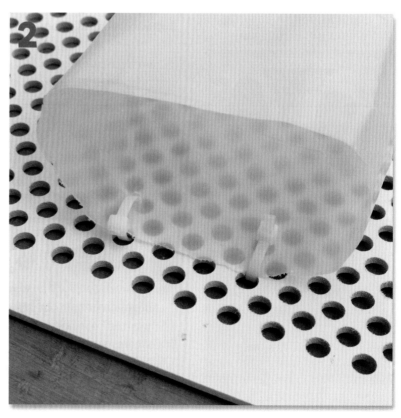

23 # Scented modelling dough

This is a wonderful sensory activity that smells divine. Children can help to knead the modelling dough and make all sorts of wonderfully scented creations when it is ready to be played with.

You will need
Saucepan
1 cup water
½ cup salt
1 tbsp vegetable oil
1 tbsp cream of tartar
Bowl
1½ cups plain flour
Water
Rolling pin
Cookie cutters
Airtight container for storage
Petals, lavender, mint
    or other herbs

1 In a saucepan mix together the water, salt, vegetable oil and cream of tartar. Heat until warm (but not boiling).

2 Remove from the heat and transfer into a bowl. Add the flour and mix together. If you're adding several different natural elements into the dough, divide it up into separate bowls.

3 Add petals, lavender, mint or other herbs and knead the mixture into a dough. If it is too sticky, add small amounts of flour and knead together. If it is too dry, add water, a tablespoon at a time, until you get the right consistency.

4 Use a rolling pin and cutters to get playing with the dough! Store in an airtight container when finished and it should keep for about a month.

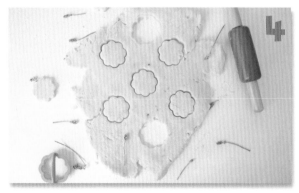

Gather a few petals, leaves and twigs for playing with the dough. They're great for creating stick faces, petal cakes or dough monsters.

You will need
500ml plastic bottle
Duct tape
3 pens
Bottle of vinegar
Baking soda
Kitchen towel
Cork (to fit bottle)

24 Easy rocket

This is a fab backyard science experiment using simple materials. If you get it right, the rocket shoots really high! While the 'making' part of this project can be done by children, the actual rocket launch should be done by an adult as the rocket is quite powerful.

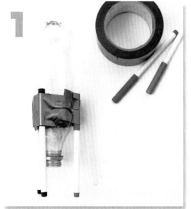

1 Open the bottle and discard the lid. Use duct tape to attach three pens around the bottle as shown in the image to make a stand for the rocket. The pens should be evenly spaced around the bottle, and at the same height so that the bottle is stable.

2 Pour about ⅓ cup of vinegar into the bottle. Place three teaspoons of baking soda in a piece of kitchen towel and roll it up tightly to create a little parcel – it needs to be small enough to fit through the rim of the bottle. Get the cork ready and check again that it fits in the bottle. It should be as loose as possible, without leaking vinegar!

3 Take the rocket and baking-soda parcel outdoors. Find a stable surface that is not obstructed by trees or other objects. Now – adults – push the baking-soda parcel into the rocket, add the cork and give it a gentle shake. Place the rocket on its legs and stand back. The rocket should foam up before zooming into space (or a short distance in the air)!

You will need
A few empty snail shells
Bucket
Old toothbrush
Water
Kitchen towel
About 4oz (100g) air-dry clay
Cocktail stick
Baking paper
Craft varnish and paintbrush

Clay snails

25

*Hunting for snail shells is all part of the fun for this project.
Just make sure they're empty or you might get a bit of a surprise
when you wash them! If you want the snails to look extra real,
you can always paint the clay dark brown once it has dried.
Then hide them somewhere if you want to create a shock...*

1 Have a look outside for some empty snail shells and collect them up in a bucket. Give them a gentle scrub in some warm water – an old toothbrush is a nice soft way to clean them. Set them aside on a piece of kitchen towel to dry.

2 Once dry, pull off a lump of air-dry clay and mould it into a sausage shape. Use dabs of water if the clay is too dry. Shape the sausage into a slug shape (ew!) and attach it to the snail shell.

3 Add two small antennae to each side of the head and press them gently in place using a cocktail stick. Place the snails gently on a place of baking paper and leave to dry overnight.

4 Gently wipe any clay marks from the shells and varnish the snails, including the shell, for a nice shiny finish.

26 Water wall

This is a really fun summer activity that uses piping, funnels and bottles to catch rainwater. Use a large piece of pegboard so the water wall can be stored away – or you could keep it all year, attached to an outside wall. Look for the materials to use in your shed, but also have a dig around for old vacuum-cleaner pipes, plastic bottles and sieves.

You will need
Piece of pegboard, at least
  3ft (1m) square in size
2 plastic milk bottles
Funnels
3 pieces of flexible pipe,
  about 3ft (1m) long
Plastic tubes
Screwdriver (or metal skewer)
Cable ties
Dish

1 Lay the pegboard flat and arrange the bottles and funnels into two or three rows on the board, working down from the top. Cut the bottom off two milk bottles and remove the lids. Start with the cut-open milk bottles and funnels at the top of the board and think about how the water will flow through when arranging the pipes and tubes. The pieces should all meet in the middle at the bottom.

2 Poke holes into one side using a screwdriver, near the bottom of each milk bottle (an adult should, of course, do this part). Use cable ties to attach the bottles onto the top of the board.

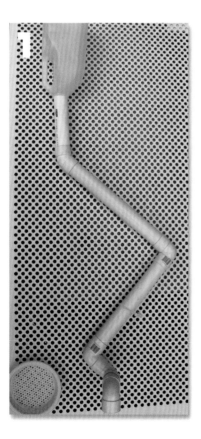

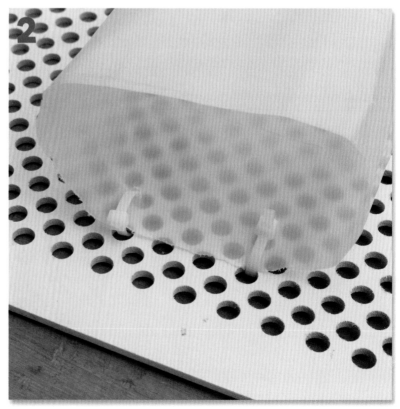

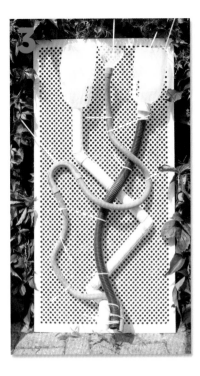

3 Tie the tubes and pipes on with cable ties. Make sure each piece connects to the one above and tie all the tubes and pipes at the bottom of the board together.

4 Prop the pegboard up and put a dish at the bottom of the board to collect the water.

Start saving bits and pieces from your recycling bin for a few weeks before you get started on this project.

27 Bubble snakes

This is a really simple and quick activity to throw together and keep the kids entertained on a sunny day – blowing the mixture through a sock makes it come out in a foamy snake of bubbles!

You will need
Scissors
500ml plastic bottle
Old adult sock
Elastic band
Bubble mixture
Liquid food colouring (optional)

1 Cut the bottom third off the plastic bottle and discard the end.

2 Pull the sock over the cut end of the bottle. Pull it up over the bottle (you can fold it up if it is too long) as far as you can go so that it is nice and tight over the end of the bottle. Secure in place with an elastic band.

3 Pour some bubble mixture into a small bowl and dip the sock end of the bottle into the solution. Blow through the top of the bottle to make a lovely snake of bubbles. If you want to make the bubbles coloured, add dabs of different colours of liquid food colouring onto the sock before dipping into the bubble solution.

Sand clay

Sand clay is a natural clay that sets hard so you can keep your sculptures. The clay has a consistency like mouldable, wet sand. Any leftover sand clay can be stored in an airtight container where it should keep for at least two weeks before it dries out.

You will need
11b 5oz (600g) play sand
5oz (150g) flour
10oz (300g) table salt
About 1 cup warm water
Rolling pin
Cookie cutters (optional)
Shells, pebbles and twigs

1 Mix together the sand, flour and salt until they are well combined. Gradually add the warm water and stir until the mixture has a dough-like consistency.

2 Tip the mixture out onto a work surface and knead a little to improve the texture of the clay.

3 Now you can mould the clay into shapes or roll it out and cut with cookie cutters, just as you would play dough. Think about things you could add to it – shells, pebbles or twigs, or turn it into silly faces or miniature sand castles. Once you're finished, leave it in a sunny spot for a day or two to set. Bear in mind the hardened clay is quite brittle and may break if handled roughly.

29

Mud alphabet

This outdoor alphabet is the perfect mixture of messy play and learning. You can buy silicone moulds from baking stores – here we've used letters but you could use any shapes you like. Head out and dig five spades full of rock- and worm-free mud.

You will need
Mud
PVA glue
Spoon and lollipop stick
Silicon letter moulds

1 Collect your mud, checking it is free from rocks and worms. Squeeze the PVA glue into the mud. Mix with a spoon and keep adding glue until the paste is the consistency of cake batter.

2 Use the spoon to scoop the mixture into the moulds and smooth it down with the lollipop stick. Pop any air bubbles and fill each mould to the top. Leave the letter moulds outside to harden overnight.

3 Once they have hardened, gently remove from the moulds and turn over to allow each letter to fully set. Make a few sets, take them outside and use them to create silly messages, or just to practise your spelling and reading.

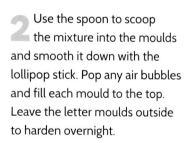

Flower ice cubes

This floral science experiment is a great way to teach children about freezing and melting. You can even freeze edible flowers, such as primroses, nasturtiums or sweet violets in ice and pop into a glass to add a pretty decoration to a summer drink.

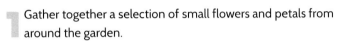

You will need
Small flowers or petals
Silicone ice-cube mould

1 Gather together a selection of small flowers and petals from around the garden.

2 Fill a silicone ice-cube mould with water and push the flowers into each cube. Pop in the freezer. Once frozen, tip the ice cubes into a bowl.

3 You can then explore playing with the ice and melting the cubes with warm water. This is a perfect way to explore nature on a hot day!

Natural clay tree face

Making a face on a tree is a fun activity kids will love to get messy with. Natural clay works best for this – see below for where to find it. If you can't find any, air-dry clay (widely available in craft stores) works just as well.

Arm yourself with a bucket and spade and some wellies – and head out to find some clay. Natural clay is fairly easy to find along the banks of a river or stream. Remember to be very careful and stick close to an adult by rivers. The clay is slippery to the touch and will often be red or grey in colour. Dig some out and if you can roll it in a sausage it will be perfect for your tree face. Keep it wet while you lug it home. Spread the clay out on a plate and remove as much of the stone and debris as you can. Make a tree face by squishing the clay onto the bark of the tree and smoothing it into shape with your fingers. Decorate the face with twigs, pebbles, feathers and sturdy leaves.

You will need
Bucket and spade
About 7oz (200g) natural
   or air-dry clay
Sticks, stones and leaves
Plate for sorting
A tree
Twigs, pebbles, feathers
   and sturdy leaves

You will need
About 1lb (500g) air-dry clay
Log of wood, chopped
    lengthways down
    the centre
Tea lights
Flowers and leaves

32 Log table decoration

Add a bit of wow to your table with this clay-covered log. Kids can be in charge of hunting out the prettiest daisies and most interesting shaped leaves. Flowers make a more eye-catching, colourful centrepiece but they will soon start to fade, so if you want your decoration to be reusable, decorate with imperishable items like shells, twigs, dried leaves or pressed flowers.

1 Spread the air-dry clay over the log. Get your fingers stuck in and smooth the clay over the top and sides of the log. Push tea lights into the clay along the top of the log and add some more clay around the edges of the lights to keep them in place.

2 Press your decorations into the clay. If you want to be able to reuse the decoration, gently remove the tea lights by wiggling them out, then set aside until the clay has dried. Once dry, pop the candles back in and your centrepiece is finished.

Colour-filled flowers

Add a hint of colour to white flowers by putting food colouring into the water. This is a fascinating science experiment that shows how water travels up the stem of a flower and into the petals, resulting in beautiful colourful flowers.

1

You will need
Scissors
Bunch of white flowers
   (carnations and roses
   work well)
Liquid food colouring
Water
3 or 4 jars
String

2

1 Cut off the bottom of the flower stems at an angle (an adult should do this bit).

2 Fill up each jar with water and food colouring in different shades. The water should be a deep colour, so keep adding food colouring until it is nice and rich.

3 Divide the flowers into the different coloured jars and tie them loosely together with string to keep them upright. Leave to sit for a few days to absorb the colour of the water. Repeat this experiment with different white flowers and see which ones work the best.

3

If you want to create individual multicoloured flowers, carefully cut the stem halfway down the middle and put each half into a jar of different coloured water.

34 Outdoor cornflower goop

This wonderful sensory activity is a really quick make that will amaze and delight! This goop is also known as 'oobleck', a term coined by Dr Seuss to describe a solid that behaves like a liquid. Tap the mixture with your fingers and it feels hard, but leave it to rest there and it will sink into the goo! You can have hours of fun.

You will need
2 cups cornflour
1 cup water
Spoon
Fresh petals, leaves and grass
Cupcake cases (optional)

To make the goop, all you need to do is pour the cornflour into a bowl then mix in the water, a little at a time until it becomes gooey. When you scrape the spoon through the mixture it should crack then quickly sink back together. Add the petals, leaves and grass on top and get playing. Try and roll the goop into shapes or serve it up in cupcake cases as delicious leafy cakes. Yum.

Poured paint pots

This is a fun way to decorate a plant pot, with a technique that even the youngest of artists can master. Acrylic paint is the best option to use for this project because it's easy to pour, it's weatherproof, and it doesn't crack once dried. Remember to cover clothes and surfaces!

You will need
Terracotta pot
Masking or painter's tape
Acrylic paint in a few colours
Plastic cups (optional)
Glitter (optional)
Baking paper (or newspaper)
Craft varnish and paintbrush

1 Cover the hole at the bottom of the pot with tape. Turn the pot upside down.

2 If the paint is very thick, thin with a little water first. You can also transfer the paint into plastic cups to make it easier to pour. Then gently pour paint, one colour at a time, over the bottom of the pot so that it trickles down the sides. Move the pot around to ensure an even coverage. You can then add glitter for a bit of extra sparkle. Transfer to a piece of baking paper to dry. When dry, remove the tape from the bottom.

3 Tidy up the rim and inside of the pot with paint. Add a coat of varnish to seal the paint and to make it durable.

36

Footprint stepping stone

A personalized stepping stone makes a lovely keepsake for the garden. The cement mixture should be made up by an adult, outside or in a well-ventilated room. You could make a stepping stone for each member of the family!

You will need
4 cups cement powder
4 cups building sand
1 cup quick-hardening cement
Water
Trowel
Old bucket
Large, flat circular plastic
    plant tray, about 12 x 2in
    (30 x 5cm) deep
About 32 plastic buttons
    (½in/1cm in diameter)
Twig

1 Begin by mixing together the cement powder with the sand in a bucket.

2 Add the hardening cement and mix together. Add water, two cups at a time, and stir with a trowel until you get a nice slurry consistency (like cake mixture). You have to be fast as the cement mixture hardens quickly!

3 Pour the mixture into the plant tray, and level the top with the back of a trowel. Leave for five minutes to set slightly. Remove shoes and socks and step into the cement to make a set of footprints. Step out gently, then wash feet to remove any cement.

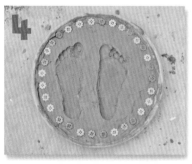

4 Decorate around the print with the plastic buttons. You can also use a twig to write your name or the date you made the stepping stone into the cement.

5 Leave the stepping stone to harden overnight. Pop out the stepping stone from the tray and place it in the garden.

Art and crafts

37

Sticky flower collage

This abstract collage is built up using fresh flowers and things found around the garden. Sticky-back plastic is a fantastic craft material that is great for instant-stick, mess-free creations.

You will need
Sticky-back plastic
Duct tape
Fresh flowers, leaves, twigs
Paper plate

1 Cut a piece of sticky-back plastic and remove the backing. Use duct tape to attach it to a wall so that the sticky side is exposed.

2 Take a walk around the garden and collect a selection of small leaves and flowers.

3 On a paper plate, sort your finds ready for sticking to the plastic. Try out different combinations of colours.

4 Attach your flowers and leaves onto the plastic to make a lovely piece of temporary art for outdoors.

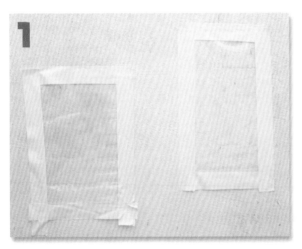

You will need
Collection of flowers, grass,
    feathers and herbs
Sturdy sticks
Strong glue
Small ball of yarn
Child-friendly paint
Paper

Natural paintbrushes

38

Painting with leaves, feathers and grass is a great way to explore different textures. See if you can find a range of things when you are outside that will produce different effects. Try to find sticks that are sturdy and long enough for little artists to grip onto.

1 Collect your natural paintbrush supplies such as flowers, grass, feathers and herbs. Make sure the flowers have long enough stems so you can attach them to a stick.

2 Glue each of the natural paintbrush heads to the end of a stick (an adult should do this bit if using a glue gun or superglue). Overlap the stems with the ends of the sticks to make the brush ends sturdy.

3 Wrap yarn around the top of the stick to cover the join between the natural paintbrush head and the stick. Secure the ends of the yarn with glue.

4 Now have fun painting with the brushes and seeing the effects produced by different brushes. Have a go at dragging, dabbing and splatting the paint onto the paper to create an abstract masterpiece.

39 Nature weaving

Nature weaving is an enjoyable activity that kids will love. Have a hunt in the garden or park for the materials. You will need four sturdy sticks for the frame and softer materials, such as long flowers, grass and feathers, for weaving. Once you've completed the weave and the flowers have wilted, you can remove them and make a fresh one.

You will need
Strong glue
4 sticks, about 12in (30cm) long
Small ball of yarn
Flowers with stems, blades of grass, twigs and feathers

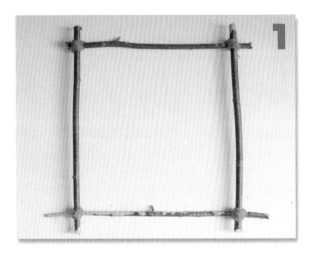

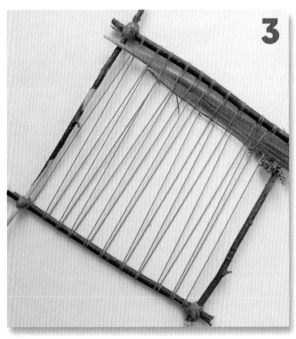

1. Begin by making the frame. Glue four sticks together in the corners to make a square. Wrap yarn around the corners to secure in place.

2. To make the weaving grid, tie yarn onto one of the top corners then pull it across to the other side of the frame. Wrap around the opposite stick, then back across the frame, working your way down the frame until you get to the bottom. Secure with a knot at the end.

3. Turn the frame so the yarn lines are vertical, then fill with flowers, grass and twigs to create a weave. To do this, weave under and over the yarn all the way from one side of the frame to the other. Repeat with the next piece, alternating between starting over or under first for each new item you weave.

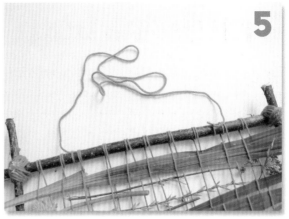

4 Fill up the frame with leaves and flowers. You don't have to start each one at the end – for smaller pieces, try starting from the middle.

5 Tie a length of yarn across the top to act as a hanging loop. Display your artwork in the garden if you wish.

40 Leaf-print bag

Leaves have a great texture for printing onto fabric, but you could also use feathers or even fruit and veg. Make sure you cover surfaces and clothes before using fabric paint, as it is very likely to stain. Collect leaves of interesting shapes, with thick veins so they leave a good imprint on the fabric.

You will need
Leaves
Kitchen paper
Old toothbrush
Sheet of newspaper
Green fabric paint
Plain piece of paper
Fine paintbrush
Plain canvas tote bag

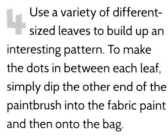

1 Remove any moisture from the leaves by blotting with kitchen paper and brush off any dirt with an old toothbrush. Then place a sheet of newspaper inside the bag to stop the fabric paint from spreading onto the back of the bag.

2 Paint your leaves with fabric paint on the bottom of the leaf (the bit with the texture on). Before printing onto the bag, use a piece of paper to practise on, testing how much paint to print onto the surface and how hard to press the leaf down.

3 When you're happy with the technique, move on to printing on the bag. When printing, place the leaf onto the bag and try not to move it around. Peel the leaf off the bag, apply more paint and repeat.

4 Use a variety of different-sized leaves to build up an interesting pattern. To make the dots in between each leaf, simply dip the other end of the paintbrush into the fabric paint and then onto the bag.

5 To seal the paint, follow the manufacturer's instructions on the fabric paint bottle.

Rainbow leaf and petal art

41

This natural rainbow has been created in summer using green leaves and colourful petals, but you could also try creating an autumn version to show the different range of colours on the leaves. If you are using petals, use ones that have fallen on the ground or you might not be in the garden owners' good books!

You will need
Double-sided tape
Blue card
Leaves and petals in lots
    of colours

Put strips of double-sided tape in three or four arc shapes onto the card, about 1in (2.5cm) apart. Head outside, armed with your card, and collect leaves and petals to fit the colours you want in your rainbow. Once your rainbow is complete, you can add little white clouds to the bottom of the picture using petals.

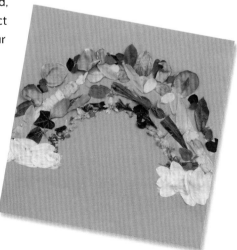

42

Twig butterflies

This simple painting activity can be done by even the littlest of artists. If you want to display your butterflies outside, cover them in sticky-back plastic before gluing on the stick bodies.

You will need
Pencil
Scissors
Coloured card
Child-friendly paint
Strong glue
Sticky-back plastic (optional)
Twigs
Pipe cleaner
Googly eyes

1 Draw and cut a butterfly shape from coloured card – make it symmetrical by folding the card and drawing on one side.

2 Splat paint onto one side of the butterfly, then fold in half down the middle and press the card down so the paint spreads.

3 Open the wings out again to create a symmetrical print, then leave to dry.

4 Cover the butterflies in sticky-back plastic for protection if you will want to take them outside. Use strong glue to attach a stick for the body of the butterfly.

5 Cut two pieces of pipe cleaner measuring about 2in (5cm) long. Curl the top of each into a circle and glue onto the back of the stick for antennae. Glue a pair of googly eyes on to finish.

Leaf rubbing

43

This is a great way to teach children about texture and a really easy way to produce an effective piece of art. Once you've finished the rubbings, you could cut out the paper leaves and turn them into home-made cards or decorative bunting.

You will need
Handful of leaves
Masking tape
Cardboard
Paper
Wax crayons

1 Collect up a handful of different leaves to rub. They should be sturdy, unbroken and uncurled. Leaves with thick veins work best for rubbing. Tape the leaves face down onto a piece of cardboard. Just use tiny pieces of masking tape to hold the leaves in place without affecting the rubbing.

2 Place the paper on top of one of the leaves and hold it steady. Rub the paper with a wax crayon, over the leaf. Hold the crayon at an angle to avoid sharp crayon marks.

3 Cover the whole paper in leaves of different shapes and colours.

Nature faces

44

This is a silly craft for kids – and one that will keep them amused more than once as you can reuse the faces. These ones have been decorated with things found in the garden, but you could also use dried foods, such as rice, lentils and pasta.

To prepare, all you need to do is draw a very simple face onto a piece of card for your kids. Then go outside with a bucket to collect any bits that could be used for hair, eyebrows, lipstick, earrings, facial hair and so on. Lay out your goodies and start decorating. Once you've finished, photograph your masterpiece, tip away the leaves and twigs and start again.

You will need
White card
Black pen
Bucket (for collection)
Twigs, leaves and petals

45 Leaf painting

This is a lovely activity to keep boredom at bay on a cold autumn afternoon. Once you've painted the leaves, you could stick them onto a large sheet of paper to create a collage.

You will need
Selection of leaves
Child-friendly colourful paints
Fine paintbrushes

Collect a handful of leaves that would make suitable canvases for your artwork – choose unbroken, dry leaves – the brown and red ones found in autumn work best. Then all you need to do is use a fine paintbrush to decorate the leaves however you like. You could paint pictures or patterns, follow the natural lines and veins of the leaves or just do something completely abstract.

Feather-print cards

You will need
3 or 4 clean feathers
Child-friendly colourful paints
Paintbrushes
Blank cards
Scrap paper

Feathers are a wonderful medium to print with as they give a lovely, delicate effect. Here we've used them to print cards, but you could also use them to create beautiful wrapping paper or gift tags. Try to use feathers of different sizes and shapes – downy ones will give a very different print to sturdier feathers.

1 Choose a feather and spread it out so that the surface, or 'vane', of the feather is separated out into several sections. This will result in a more interesting print. Apply a thin layer of paint to the surface with a paintbrush.

2 Place the feather face down onto the front of the card, being careful not to move it around. Take the piece of scrap paper and place it on top of the feather. Press down firmly, then remove.

3 Gently peel away the feather. You can then experiment on scrap paper with different feathers and try combining different colours onto one feather to get different effects.

Pine-cone wreath

47

This is a great activity with two elements to it - firstly shaking pine cones in a box of paint to make them multicoloured, then turning your pine cones into a beautiful wreath! You could just do the first part if you can't find enough pine cones to create the wreath.

You will need

Sticky tape
Sheet of plain paper
Old box or tray with sides
(which will get covered
in paint!)
Child-friendly paints in
a variety of colours

About 40 pine cones
Foam board (optional)
Strong glue
String
Masking tape

1 Tape plain paper into the bottom of your box or tray.

2 Squirt paint into the bottom of the tray. Throw the pine cones in, then give the box a shake.

3 Squeeze more paint onto the pine cones and shake some more to build up the colours. Remove the pine cones from the box and leave to dry.

4 To turn the pine cones into a wreath, draw and cut a ring shape onto foam board (11in/28cm wide and a ring thickness of 2in/5cm). Paint the front and sides in your favourite colour and leave to dry.

5 Glue the pine cones onto the ring. Once dry, tape a length of string onto the back of the wreath for hanging.

The paper at the bottom of the box will have a really cool random print on it that you could turn into cards or wrapping paper.

48 Mud paint

This is a fun way to mix painting with playing outdoors. This project is as much about having fun creating the mud paint as it is painting with it. You could use the natural paintbrushes on page 65 to create your masterpieces.

You will need
Bucket and spade
Soil
Muffin tray (or small pots)
Water
Liquid food colouring
Thick card

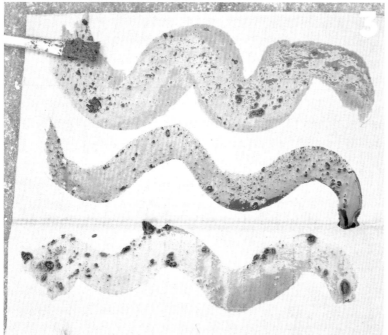

1 Get a bucket and spade and get digging in the garden to collect your soil. Make sure there are no stones, twigs or worms in there! Pop the soil into the muffin tray and mix with a small amount of water until you get a paste.

2 Add liquid food colouring to the paste and mix in. The more you add, the brighter the colour will be.

3 Use your mud paint to get painting on thick card.

Autumn-leaf bowl

49

This bowl is made entirely out of leaves! Take a carrier bag next time you're out on a walk to collect lots of leaves. This craft is best done in autumn, when leaves are brown and crunchy and don't have a lot of moisture in them. To make a sturdy bowl you'll need several layers of leaves.

You will need
Balloon
PVA glue and paintbrush
Brown leaves (a carrier-bag full)
Scissors

1 Blow up the balloon and cover the top third of it with PVA glue. Arrange the leaves onto the glue, making sure there are no gaps. Add another layer of glue on top of the leaves to stick them down.

2 Leave to dry overnight and then repeat steps 1 and 2 to add another two or three layers of leaves.

3 Once all the layers are dry, pop the balloon and remove from the bowl. You can neaten up the rim of the bowl using scissors, as we have done, or leave it natural.

50 Spooky spiderweb cards

This is a simple but effective way to create a beautiful piece of art from a real spiderweb. Bear in mind this project involves using spray paint, which should be done with close adult supervision.

1

You will need
Black card (cut into squares to fit
    the blank cards)
White or silver spray paint
Scissors
Sticky-back plastic
Glue
Blank cards
Pens

2

1 Begin by getting outside, with your black card and spray paint, to find suitable spiderwebs. Pick webs that no longer have spiders inhabiting them. Make sure any paint sprayed would not go onto surfaces, then spray the web with the paint. Put the card behind the painted web and pull it forward so that the web pattern is collected onto the card.

2 Cut pieces of sticky-back plastic and place them gently onto the card, pressing down firmly to seal. If you like you can just select parts of the spider web that worked best rather than cover the whole card.

3

3 Glue the spiderwebs onto the blank cards, allowing space for a little message at the top.

Look out for
spiderwebs on tree
branches and in sheltered
corners outside.

Twig star garden decorations

These decorations are a brilliant way of using up old plastic carrier bags. They're waterproof so can be hung outside as a lovely garden decoration, but you could switch the plastic bags for tissue paper if you want to hang them up indoors instead.

1 Take five twigs and cut them all to the same length. Secateurs are good for this – with an adult's help – but you could use scissors or just snap them to size.

2 Arrange the twigs on a piece of newspaper to create a star shape, then glue together and leave to set. Repeat to make a collection of different-sized stars.

3 Cut the plastic bags into roughly 1in (2.5cm)-sized squares. Mix them up and place them in a bowl. Cut a piece of sticky-back plastic that is just slightly larger than one of your stars, peel off the backing and cover it with coloured squares to create a plastic mosaic.

4 Glue the plastic onto the star with the squares at the back, then trim the plastic to the size of the star.

5 Thread string onto one corner of each star you have made and hang your decorations in the garden.

You will need
Selection of sturdy twigs
Secateurs
Scissors
Newspaper
Glue
Old plastic bags – colourful
    ones are best
Bowl
Sticky-back plastic
String

52 Solar-print notebooks

Solar printing is a fun, easy and mess-free way for kids to create personalized prints during the summer. Solar print paper is photosensitive and changes colour when left in the sunshine, enabling you to create interesting shapes by leaving objects on top of it. Bear in mind that things that lie flat will create the best prints. You can buy solar paper online in packs.

1 Collect some things from outside that have an interesting shape: leaves, feathers and flower petals work well. Place the solar paper onto a piece of corrugated card. Arrange your nature finds on top of the paper. Place a piece of acetate or cling film over the top and secure it in place with drawing pins along the edge of the card. Take the collage outside and place it in the sunshine.

2 Follow the guidelines on the packet for how long to keep the paper exposed for (as this will vary depending on the paper), then remove the acetate or cling film and nature finds.

3 Rinse the paper in cold water for about a minute.

4 Leave the paper to dry flat.

5 To make the notebook, stack eight sheets of coloured paper together with the solar paper on top. Cut the coloured paper to the same size as the solar paper, if required. Fold the stack in half to resemble a book.

6 Staple the book together on the fold and add decorative tape down the fold to cover the staples and add a spine.

You will need

Leaves, flowers and feathers
Solar print paper
Piece of corrugated card
Sheet of clear acetate or cling film
Drawing pins
8 sheets of coloured paper
Scissors
Stapler
Decorative tape

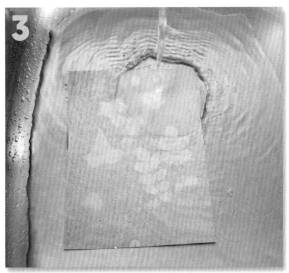

53 Land art

You don't have to always take a bucket and spade when you go down to the beach – you could also get creative with the materials you find around the shore to create your own giant picture. We've made a mermaid here to fit with the beach setting, but you can always create an abstract piece of art or even use the materials to practise spelling out words.

You will need
Stones
Shells
Seaweed
Twigs

Begin by gathering all the materials you need and evening out the sand with you hands to give a nice flat canvas. Then begin to build up your picture, starting with the outline, then filling in the shape with colour and texture. It's a good idea to stand back and look at your work regularly so you can see the whole thing taking shape.

Dream catcher

This dream catcher is made from the centre part of an embroidery hoop, which you can find in most craft stores. A dream catcher is traditionally woven to resemble a spider's web. You will need some feathers, which you can search for on a woodland walk, and some beads to decorate.

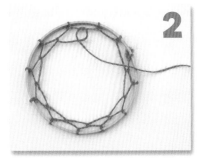

You will need
2 shades of brightly coloured twine
Embroidery hoop
Different-coloured beads
6 feathers
Glue

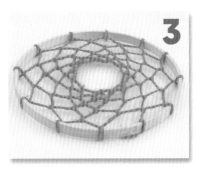

1 To make the weave on the embroidery hoop, begin by tying the end of the twine onto the hoop. Pull the twine about 1½in (4cm) along and fold it over the top of the hoop from the front. Bring the twine in through the loop and pull tight. Continue all the way along the hoop.

2 When you get to the beginning, continue to loop the twine and go forward, but instead of looping around the hoop, loop through the previous row of twine, in the centre of each loop. Pull tight each time.

3 Keep going round, looping and pulling tight, until the gaps become too small to continue easily. Tie the twine in the centre and trim the loose ends.

4 Tie three pieces of twine onto the bottom of the hoop, evenly spaced out. Add beads to each one, then cut to your preferred lengths (this one was about 10in/25cm in the centre). Glue two feathers onto the bottom of each piece of twine. Add another length of twine to the top of the hoop to enable you to hang your dream catcher.

Games

55 # Tic-tac-toe

This is a lovely natural version of the classic game, also known as noughts and crosses. An adult will need to cut the branch into counters, although painted pebbles, cork coasters, pine cones or shells could be used instead.

1

You will need
Branch, about 1½in (4cm) thick
Saw
Child-friendly paints
Paintbrushes
Masking tape
Pencil with a rubber end
4 long twigs

2

1 Cut the branch into 12 counters about ½in (1cm) thick. Paint half the counters – they can be any pattern and colour you like, as long as they are all the same. To make stripes, add thin strips of masking tape onto half the counters. Paint, then remove the strips once dry.

2 To make the remaining counters spotty, dip the rubber end of a pencil lightly into paint and use it to stamp spots on the wood.

3 When your counters are ready, head outside and look for four long twigs to create the classic 3 x 3 square grid. To play the game, two players take it in turns to place their counters on the grid. The first person who can get three of their counters in a row in any direction is the winner.

Take the counters with you on a woodland walk, then the kids can hunt for suitable twigs for the grid and play the game while out and about.

Colour hunt

This colour-hunt game is simple to set up and will keep the kids entertained and exploring outside. Make a sheet for each child taking part – and see who can fill up their colours the quickest.

You will need
Scissors
Sheet of white card
Pencil and ruler
Felt-tip pens
Doubled-sided tape
Clipboard (optional)

1 Cut the card in half lengthways then draw a table with two columns and six to ten rows. Each row will represent a colour to be found, so the more you add the longer the game will take.

2 Use felt-tip pens to colour the boxes on the left. Add a few strips of double-sided tape to the boxes on the right.

3 When you're ready, peel off the tape and get hunting for colours! Go outside with your chart (on a clipboard is easiest) and see what you can find in nature that matches your colours. Stick anything you find onto the tape in the chart.

57 Find the pebbles

This pebble hunt is a fun way to mix nature, learning and craft. Collect pebbles or stones next time you're at the beach or park. If you collect enough, you could even do the whole alphabet!

You will need
Pebbles
Acrylic paints
Paintbrushes
Craft varnish

1 Paint your pebbles an array of colours. You may need a few coats to get a good coverage. Leave to dry.

2 Use the paint to write letters or numbers onto the pebbles. Cover with a coat of varnish.

3 Head outside and hide the pebbles. Have fun trying to find them, then try putting them into numerical order or spelling out words.

Pressed flower pairs game

This is a garden version of the classic pairs game, featuring flowers and leaves. To play, shuffle the cards and place them face down on the table. Players take it in turn to pick two cards, trying to remember the location of the different cards. If you find a pair, pick them up and keep them. The player with the most pairs wins.

58

You will need
Selection of flowers
  and leaves
2 pieces plain paper
Flower press (or heavy books)
2 sheets of A4 yellow card
Sticky-back plastic
Scissors

1 Begin by collecting a selection of flowers and leaves for your game. Try to select small flowers that are not too bulky, and go for ones that are don't look similar to the other pairs collected. You will need two of each kind, and about 20 pairs in total.

2 Place the flowers, face down, between two small pieces of plain paper. Place this into a flower press. If you don't have a press, place the flowers inside a heavy book, with other books stacked on top. Leave for at least a week before opening up.

3 Divide a piece of coloured card into a grid with 20 boxes measuring 2 x 2½in (5 x 6cm). Place the flowers onto the grid, face up, in their pairs.

4 Carefully cover the cards with sticky-back plastic. Press down well to seal.

5 Cut out the squares to make your cards.

89

59 Tin-can bowling

This is a great outdoor project that recycles old tin cans and turns them into a garden bowling game. It's very easy to make and the tins can be decorated however you like.

Remove all the labels, then clean and dry the cans. Paint each one a different colour or leave them unpainted if you prefer. You could also decorate them with stickers or coloured tape for a really quick make. To play, line four of them next to each other, then stack the remaining cans on top to make a pyramid. Take a few steps back, roll the ball and see how many you can knock over.

You will need
10 tin cans
Acrylic paints
Paintbrushes
Stickers or coloured tape
Tennis ball

Outdoor games

There are loads of really simple games that you can play outdoors with little resources or set up. All you need is space, energy and willing kids to get involved! Here are a few to get you started:

Sack races (2+ players) You don't need to buy sacks – you can use bin bags or old pillow cases. All you need is a start and finish line. You could also try to do three-legged races and egg and spoon races, and hold your own mini sports day!

Marbles (2+ players) is a traditional game for kids. In this version, mark out a ring in chalk or string on the pavement, or on the grass, with a start line just outside the ring. Place about 10 marbles in the ring. Players then take it in turns to roll their 'shooter' marble (a slightly larger marble) in from the start line to try and knock as many marbles as you can out of the ring – each one you hit out, you keep. The winner is the one with the most marbles collected at the end of the game.

Limbo (3+ players) is a really easy game to do anywhere. Hunt for a big stick and have two people holding it at each end. Then take it in turns to wiggle under the stick without falling over! Lower the stick each time to make it harder.

Shadow tag (4+ players) is a sunny-day chase game. One person, the tagger, has to chase the other players. If they touch their shadow that person then becomes the tagger.

Stuck in the mud (4+ players) is another chase game. One person has to try and tag the other people in the game. If they manage to tag someone, that person has to stand still with their legs open until another player crawls underneath to free them. The winner is the last person to be tagged.

Catch the flag (6+ players) is a team game where you have to capture the opposite team's flag to win. Divide your players into two teams, each with a flag (or distinctive object) in a territory (a marked-off area). Teams must try to get the other team's flag and return it to their own territory. Players from the opposite team can be tagged and sent to jail if they are in your territory. They can be freed by being tagged by their team mates.

Snakes in the grass (6+ players) Work out a boundary for the game, then select two players to be 'snakes'. The snakes have to try and tag the players, but they can only crawl on their hands and needs. If someone is tagged or leaves the boundary area, they become a snake too.

61 Twig marble run

Kids often come home from the park with pockets full of twigs, so why not put them to good use by turning them into a marble run? All you need is a lid of a shoebox plus some marbles and you can make a fantastic little game that's great for taking on car journeys. You don't just have to use twigs to create these runs – you could also use bamboo or straws, with pebbles, acorns or shells for dead ends.

You will need
Child-friendly paints in various colours
Paintbrushes
Lid of a box (a shoe-box lid works well)
Pencil, ruler and rubber
Marbles
Thin twigs (or bamboo or straws)
Pebbles, acorns or shells (for dead ends)
Strong glue
Stickers
Craft varnish and paintbrush

1 Paint the box using nice bright colours and leave to dry. Mark out the channels of a maze with pencil as shown. The lines should be at least 1½in (4cm) wide to allow you to fit a marble in once the twigs are in place. Add a few dead ends too.

2 Paint the twigs in a contrasting colour to the box and leave to dry. Glue the twigs onto the maze along the pencil marks.

3 Decorate the marble run with stickers and add a coat of varnish to seal everything in place.

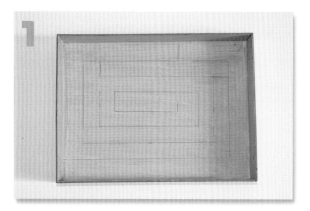

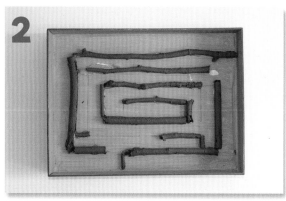

Nature-tray game

This simple memory game can be played anywhere, requires very little set up and you can do it with any objects small enough to fit on the tray. Kids also love being the one to remove the items and challenge adults to remember what was on the tray.

You will need
A tray
Nature finds, such as pine cones, stones,
    flowers, grass, sticks and feathers
Tea towel

Go for a short walk outdoors and find a selection of different items that will fit onto your tray. The game works best with about 10 objects, but you can add more as you go along to make it more difficult. Lay the objects out on a tray and cover it up with a tea towel. Sit the children around the tray and remove the cloth for one minute so that they can study the contents and try to remember them. Then children must cover their eyes while one or two items are removed from the tray. Who can remember which items have been taken away?

To make the game harder, you can either add more things to the tray to be remembered, or give a shorter amount of studying time.

Rainy day

63 Pressed-flower tea light

This pretty flower light can add a bit of sparkle to a garden at night-time or be used as a night light.

You will need
Flowers for pressing
2 pieces of plain paper
Flower press (or heavy books)
PVA glue
Paintbrush
Clear jar (labels removed
    and clean)
Glitter
Battery-operated tea light
String (optional)

1 Place the flowers, face down, between two pieces of paper and place into a flower press. If you don't have a press, place inside a heavy book, with other books stacked on top. Leave for at least a week.

2 Once the flowers have been pressed, spread a thin layer of glue on the inside of the jar with a paintbrush.

3 Carefully place the flowers onto the glued surface inside the jar, with the tops of the flowers facing out. Add a layer of glue onto the back of the flowers to keep them in place.

4 While the glue is tacky, sprinkle glitter into the inside of the jar, then leave the glue to dry. Pop your tea light in.

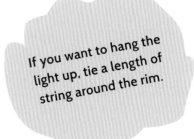

If you want to hang the light up, tie a length of string around the rim.

Weather chart

You can do as many segments as you like for this chart, for as many different types of weather you can think of! This is a great way to get children learning about the weather and how quickly it changes, and this simple chart could be adapted to create all sorts of other charts such as days of the week, or months.

You will need
2 paper plates
Ruler and pencil
Black permanent marker
Scissors
Child-friendly paints
Scissors
Split pin

1. Divide the back of one of the paper plates into five (or more) equal segments and draw them on the plate using a black marker pen. For the other plate, divide it up as before but only mark out one segment, and just mark this segment as far as the rim. Carefully cut the segment out, leaving the rim of the plate in place, to create a window.

2. Paint each of the segments on the uncut plate with various weather types – you can label them too if you like. Paint only down to the rim of the plate.

3. Paint the other plate a plain colour and leave to dry. If you want to, use the black marker pen to label the chart with the words, 'Today it is...' just above the cut-out window.

4. With the window plate on top, push a split pin through the centre of both plates and secure at the back. Give the plates a little wiggle to loosen them up and your weather chart is complete. Move the plate round to show the day's weather in the cut-out segment.

65 # Star-gazing sewing cards

This is a lovely way to help children develop their first sewing skills. Head outside on a clear evening, look up to the stars and see what constellations you can identify. You can look up which ones can be seen from your area on the internet first to get an idea.

You will need
A4 sheet of black card
Scissors
Long-reach hole punch
   (or craft knife)
Chopping board (optional)
Small ball of yarn
Large plastic needle
Sticky tape

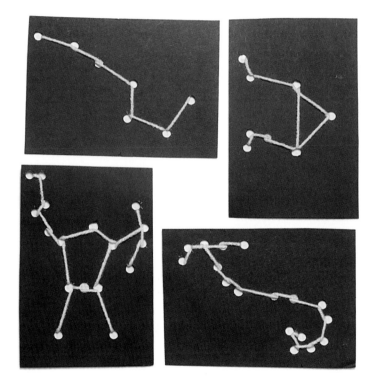

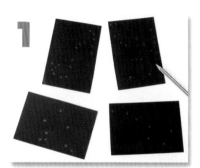

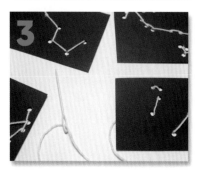

1 Fold and cut the card into four smaller pieces. Decide which groups of stars you would like to stitch – these could be ones you can see from your house, your star sign or just the ones you like best. Look them up on the internet and mark the points onto each of the cards.

2 Make holes where marked using a hole punch or – very carefully – with a craft knife on a chopping board.

3 Thread about a yard (metre) of yarn onto the needle. Tape one end onto the back of the card and stitch the constellations onto the sewing cards. Stitch all the way around the constellation and then back again so that the yarn is visible between every point. Seal the end once more with tape.

Matchbox bird box

This little bird box can be used to store tiny trinkets, or you could just hang it up to look decorative.

1

2

3

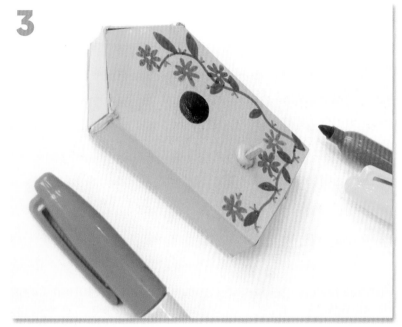

You will need
Large matchbox
Scissors
Scrap of card
Glue
Match
Child-friendly pale pink
    and yellow paint
Paintbrushes
Coloured marker pens

1 Slide the lid off the matchbox and cut off the ends to form a roof-shaped point. Place the box back inside and trim the corners to the same size.

2 Cut ¾in (2cm) off the end of a match and glue it near the bottom of the matchbox to create a perch.

3 Cut a strip of card to fit over the top of the roof and glue on top. Paint the outside of the box pink and the inside yellow, then leave to dry. Use marker pens to decorate the bird box with flowers, leaves or patterns.

67 Rose-petal perfume

This perfume is easy to make and is kind to the skin. Roses smell particularly wonderful, but you could also use other fragrant garden flowers or herbs, such as lavender or mint. Save old perfume bottles or small plastic ones (such as sample toiletry bottles) in preparation for this project.

 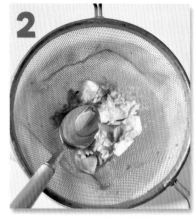 

You will need
2 cups water
Saucepan
Petals from 3 roses in
    any colour
Strainer
Pink food colouring and
    glitter (optional)
Bottle
Small funnel

1 Heat the water in a pan to a low boil, then remove from the heat. Place the petals into the water and push them under. Leave the water to cool.

2 Use a strainer to transfer the water into a bowl and strain any liquid out of the petals. You can add a drop of pink food colouring and some glitter at this point if you'd like to make your perfume an appealing colour. Only add a tiny amount of food colouring to create a hint of pink – if you add too much it may stain the skin.

3 Transfer the perfume into a bottle using a funnel.

Mermaid mirror

All wannabe mermaids need a mirror to admire themselves in – and using shells collected from a trip to the seaside is the perfect material to decorate a mirror. Small mirrors are easy to get hold of from craft shops, but you could also use tinfoil if you aren't too worried about the reflection.

68

You will need
Pencil
Scissors
Corrugated card, about 10 x 10in (25 x 25cm)
Small oval mirror (or piece of tinfoil), 1½ x 2½in (4 x 6cm)
PVA glue
Child-friendly blue paint
Paintbrush
Glitter
Strong glue
Shells
Sequins

1 Use the template below to draw and cut two mirror shapes on corrugated card. On one of the pieces of card, draw around the real mirror and cut out. This will be where the mirror slots into.

2 Glue the two pieces of card together and paint them. Glue the mirror into the cut-out section on the front. Carefully spread PVA glue around the edge of the mirror and sprinkle glitter over the edges.

3 Using strong glue, stick the shells and sequins around the mirror to decorate.

Mirror template
Photocopy at 200%

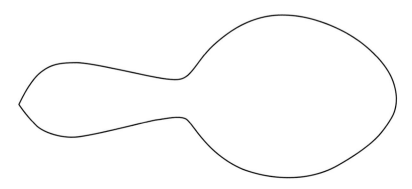

69 Lavender pouches

These fragrant hearts make a lovely gift for friends and family. They can be any shape you like, or you can even make a little lavender pillow for a teddy. First you need to collect some fresh lavender from the garden. Leave it on a tray in a warm spot for a few weeks to dry before you use it for this project.

You will need
Cotton heart template
Scissors
Cotton fabric
Sewing pins
Embroidery thread
   and needle
Sewing machine (optional)
Sprigs of dried lavender
Spoon
10in (25cm) thin ribbon
Button

1 Use the template to cut two hearts from the cotton fabric. Pin the fabric right sides together and sew by hand or on a sewing machine all the way round, ¼in (5mm) from the edge. Leave a 1½in (4cm) gap for turning.

2 Using the scissors, make snips around the seam in the curved edges to prevent puckering.

3 Turn the material right-side out and push the corners out with your fingers or the points of the scissors.

4 Remove the petals from the stems of lavender and use a spoon to fill the heart with them. Sew up the turning gap.

5 Fold the ribbon in half, then sew in place onto the top of the heart. Sew a button onto the top.

102

Heart template

Photocopy at 200%

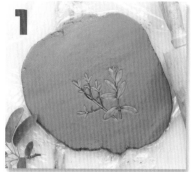

(70) Leaf-print bowl

Air-dry clay is a great medium for kids to play with. It's cheap, easy to work with and great fun to paint. Varnishing the bowl is optional but will make it stronger and more resistant to moisture and dirt.

You will need
Leaves
About 10oz (300g)
   air-dry clay
Cling film
Rolling pin

Saucer
Small bowl with water
Craft varnish and paintbrush
   (optional)

1 Collect up a few leaves – those attached to small branches with thin stems work best for printing. Place your clay on a piece of cling film and roll out to about ¼in (5mm). Arrange your leaves on top and roll over the clay again to create an imprint. Gently peel away the leaves.

2 Place a saucer on top of the clay over the leaf prints. Cut around it and remove the excess. Smooth the clay with your fingers dipped into a little water.

3 Lift up the clay using the cling film and place it in the bowl, with the cling film still underneath. Press down into the bowl and set aside to dry for at least 24 hours.

4 If you wish, add a lick of varnish using a paintbrush to give your bowl a nice shiny finish.

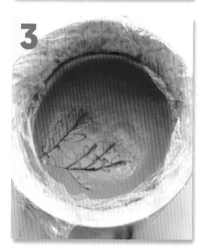

Pressed-flower bookmarks

Turning pressed flowers into bookmarks is a lovely way to keep and display them. Find a bucket and go on a hunt for some flowers to press – it's all part of the fun! Small, delicate flowers are best for this project: daisies and buttercups are perfect. Pick a few small leaves too for greenery. After picking, press the flowers as quickly as you can before they wilt.

1 Place the flowers, face down, between two small pieces of blotting paper. Place this into a flower press, or, if you do not have one you can put them into a heavy book, with other books stacked on top. Leave for a week before opening it all out again.

2 Cut a bookmark shape from a piece of card. Cut the centre out to create a frame that is about ¼in (5mm) wide.

3 Place the bookmark onto a piece of sticky-back plastic. Put the flowers, face down, inside the frame. Place another sheet of plastic on top to seal the flowers in and press down. Cut out the bookmark, leaving a small border of plastic around the card to keep it stuck together.

You will need
Small flowers
Blotting paper
Flower press or heavy books
A4 sheet of coloured card
Sticky-back plastic
Scissors

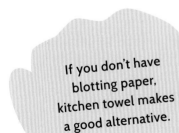
If you don't have blotting paper, kitchen towel makes a good alternative.

72 Scented soaps

These home-made aromatic soaps would make a lovely gift and are easier to create than you might think. These ones are lavender and thyme, but you could also make soaps using dried rose petals, lemon and mint, or poppy seeds for an exfoliating version.

You will need
Garden herbs, such as lavender, cotton lavender and thyme
About 18oz (500g) clear soap
Jug (suitable for microwave)
Lavender essential oil (optional)
Loose-bottom cake tin
Palette knife
Cookie cutter
Baking paper

1 Collect bunches of garden herbs (ask an adult first!) You will need about two cups' worth. Pull apart into small pieces, removing any woody bits.

2 Chop the soap into 1in (2.5cm) sized chunks and place into a jug. Put in the microwave and heat in 30-second blasts until the soap has melted. Add a few drops of essential oil and stir in, if using.

3 Sprinkle the herbs into the cake tin and gently pour the soap on top. Leave to set for at least two hours.

4 Use a palette knife to loosen the edge of the soap from the tin then pop it out. If there are bubble marks on the top, rinse the giant soap in warm water and rub the surface with your fingers until smooth.

5 Use a cookie cutter to cut out shapes from the soap. Avoid waste by keeping the shapes as close together as possible. Wrap the soap in baking paper with a stick of lavender on top for the perfect gift.

Bottle-top bugs

This ladybird, bluebottle fly and spider are super-simple makes from some old plastic bottle tops. If you like, you can glue magnets onto the bottom of the bugs once you're finished, to turn them into wiggly-jiggly fridge magnets!

1

2

3

You will need
Red, blue and black bottle tops
Black permanent pen
Craft glue
Googly eyes
10 black pipe cleaners
Old plastic carrier bags
Fridge magnets (optional)

1 Use a black permanent pen to mark the features of a ladybird onto the red bottle top. Then glue googly eyes onto each bottle top.

2 Turn the bottle tops upside down and glue three pipe cleaners into the red and blue bottle tops, and four pipe cleaners onto the black bottle top. Spread the pipe cleaners out and bend to look like legs. Leave them to dry, then trim them to size.

3 Cut a scrap of plastic from a carrier bag. Fold it in half and cut two wing shapes into the fold. Glue two pairs of small wings onto the centre of the ladybird and two bigger pairs onto the bluebottle. Glue on fridge magnets if you wish.

74 Tree-stump key rings

Old bits of branch from softwoods can make lovely key rings with a little bit of TLC. An adult will need to cut small segments of the branch off with a saw in preparation for this craft.

You will need
1½–3in (4–8cm) branch, cut
    into ½in (2cm) thick pieces
Sandpaper
Acrylic paint and fine
    paintbrush
Hand drill and 5mm drill bit
Craft varnish and paintbrush
Key ring

1 Sand the pieces of wood with a piece of sandpaper until they are lovely and smooth.

2 Use a fine paintbrush to paint simple pictures onto the wood – you could paint your house, your favourite thing or even a self-portrait.

3 Drill a hole into the top of the wood, about ¼in (5mm) from the edge. Add a coat of varnish and leave to dry before attaching the key ring.

Clothes-peg animals

These little peg creatures are really quick and easy to make. They are made from craft foam and acrylic paint so that they can be used outdoors, but if you're keeping them in the house you could use coloured card and child-friendly paint instead. If you do use acrylic paint, make sure to cover clothes and surfaces before starting the craft because it won't wash out.

You will need
Acrylic paint (or child-friendly paint) in a variety of colours
Wooden clothes pegs
Craft foam (or card) in a variety of colours
Black permanent pen
Craft glue
Washing line
Fridge magnets (optional)

1 Begin by painting the pegs all over to create a base colour for each animal. Here we've gone for frog green, lion yellow, elephant grey and panda white. Leave to dry.

2 Draw and cut the shapes for your animals from craft foam. Use the pictures as a guideline, or create your own. Cut a head and body piece, then any extra pieces for your animal, such as tails, tummies and so on.

3 Add features to the foam using the black marker pen, then glue the shapes onto the pegs. Glue tails onto the back. Once dry, simply pop them on the washing line to brighten up your garden. If you prefer, glue magnets to the back of each peg and use them as fridge magnets.

76 Leaf punching

This is a fun activity that uses leaves collected from an outdoor adventure. You could even save the punched-out part of the leaves in a little envelope for your very own nature confetti.

Collect a selection of leaves in different sizes, then simply use the hole punch to make patterns. If you want them to be symmetrical, fold the leaf in half before punching. When you've finished, you could string the leaves together to make bunting.

You will need
Leaves
Patterned hole punch
Envelope (optional)

77 Fruit and veg markers

This craft turns cheap throwaway wooden spoons into beautiful markers for your little vegetable patch (take a look at the mini patch on page 35 for inspiration). This project uses acrylic paints and varnish to ensure the pictures stay put in all weathers, so be sure to cover up clothing and surfaces.

You will need
Pencil
A selection of small,
    disposable wooden
    spoons
Acrylic paint and fine
    paintbrushes
Craft varnish and paintbrush

1 Use a pencil to sketch simple pictures of your fruit and veg onto the back of each wooden spoon, then use acrylic paints to fill in the pictures. Leave to dry before adding a slick of varnish to seal and make weatherproof.

2 Place each marker in the ground to identify the vegetables growing in your patch.

Sycamore spinner

Sycamore seeds are fantastic for crafting and can be turned into lots of things, such as this colourful spinner to cheer up your garden. Go on a hunt for the winged seeds from sycamore trees when you're next out for a woodland walk.

78

You will need
About 25 sycamore seeds
Child-friendly paint in a
     variety of colours
Paintbrushes
Small piece of corrugated
     card
Pencil
8in (20cm) length of dowel
Decorative tape
Strong glue
Split pin
Varnish

1 Begin by painting the sycamore seeds in a variety of bright colours. You will need several coats to get a good coverage.

2 Cut a circle from corrugated card 2½in (6cm) in diameter. Use a pencil or pen to poke a small hole in the middle and paint one side a nice bright colour. Cover the piece of dowel in decorative tape.

3 Glue the seeds around the cardboard circle, avoiding the hole in the centre.

4 Push the split pin through the hole and fold the ends around the top of the dowel. Give the spinner part a lick of varnish to protect from the elements.

79 Mint lip balm

Grow your own mint leaves and use them to make a lip-soothing balm. Save old lip balm containers for reuse in this project, or buy new ones online or from a pharmacy.

You will need
5 mint leaves
Pestle and mortar
4 tbsp petroleum jelly
Vanilla or peppermint extract
4 small plastic containers
Funnel

1 Tear the mint leaves into small pieces and use a pestle and mortar to pound into a fine mush.

2 Place the petroleum jelly into a microwavable bowl. Heat in a microwave in 20-second bursts until it has melted to a liquid, then stir the mint leaves into the mixture. Add a drop or two of peppermint or vanilla extract into the mixture.

3 Using the funnel, pour the mixture into the pots. Pop in the freezer for half an hour to firm up, or leave out to set naturally.

!

Be very careful with hot liquids.

Wind chimes

These chimes are made using old metal spoons and keys, and they make a surprisingly beautiful sound when tinkling in the wind. You could use other objects for your wind chimes, as long as they are made from metal and can be hung easily – bottle caps, ring pulls or even nuts and bolts will work.

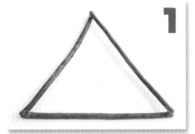

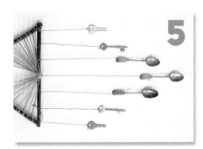

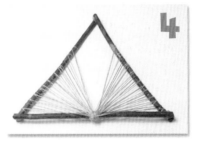

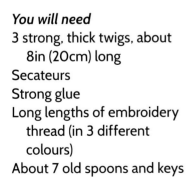

1 Ask an adult to cut all the twigs to the same length with the secateurs and glue together to form a triangle. Leave to dry.

2 Use embroidery thread to decorate the triangle. For this pattern, start by tying the embroidery thread onto the centre of one of the twigs. Pull it taut and loop the thread onto one side of the triangle, about a quarter of the way down from the top.

3 Bring the thread back down to the first knot and loop round it. Repeat this process two more times, each time going a little lower along the twig.

4 Repeat step 3 using the two other colours of thread.

5 Use more embroidery thread to tie spoons and old keys (make sure they're no longer in use!) at different lengths onto the bottom of the triangle. They should be close enough to just touch each other in a breeze. Hang outside in a sheltered area and enjoy the sweet sound of your chimes!

You will need
3 strong, thick twigs, about 8in (20cm) long
Secateurs
Strong glue
Long lengths of embroidery thread (in 3 different colours)
About 7 old spoons and keys

Food and drink

81

Home-grown pizza toppings

This spring activity is a great way to encourage children to eat herbs and vegetables and get them interested in gardening. You could use the mini vegetable planter from page 35 or a large pot to grow your chosen veggies in.

First of all, decide what you would like to have on your pizza. You could have tomatoes, basil and spring onions, as shown here, or incorporate other herbs and leaves such as chives, rosemary, rocket and spinach. Follow the guide on the seed packet: you may need to grow the seeds in newspaper pots first, until they sprout into seedlings. Then fill your pot with compost and add the seeds or seedlings. Place them in a sunny spot, water regularly and watch them grow!

You will need
Seeds for growing (see left)
Large plant pot or wooden crate
Compost
Newspaper seedling pots (see page 29)

82

S'mores

S'mores are a yummy outdoor treat when camping or having an outdoor party. Try experimenting with different types of chocolate or, for an extra indulgence, use chocolate-topped biscuits. Delicious!

You will need
For each s'more
3 or 4 squares of chocolate
2 plain biscuits
1 large marshmallow or several small ones
Tinfoil

1 Place small chunks of chocolate and marshmallows onto one of the biscuits. Press the other biscuit on top to create a 'sandwich', then wrap in tinfoil.

2 Put on a campfire, under a grill or in a pan to heat up for about five minutes, until the chocolate and marshmallows are deliciously gooey.

3 Unwrap your s'mores, let them cool a little and enjoy.

Chocolate-dipped apples

83

These apples are a delicious sweet snack. Pick apples straight off the tree and get chocolate dipping.

You will need
4 sweet apples
Lollipop sticks
3½oz (100g) each of milk
   and white chocolate
Sprinkles (hundreds and
   thousands)
Finely chopped nuts, seeds
   and shredded coconut
Baking tray with baking paper
Makes 4

1 Twist and remove the apple stalks and push the lollipop stick into the core.

2 Break the white and milk chocolate into small pieces and put into separate glass bowls. Place one of the bowls over a pan of boiling water and stir until melted – ask an adult to help with this part. Dip the apple into the bowl and give it a twist to coat it in chocolate. Repeat with the other bowl of chocolate.

3 Tip the sprinkles and nuts onto a baking tray and dip the chocolate apples into the mixture. Pop into the fridge to harden. You can drizzle more chocolate onto your apples once the first layer has hardened if you like.

84

Forager's crumble

This delicious crumble is really simple to make and works with lots of fruits you can find easily in the garden or out in the countryside, such as apples, blackberries and rhubarb.

You will need
1lb 5oz (600g) foraged fruits
Pie dish
2–3 tbsp sugar (for the filling)
1 tbsp water
Cling film
2oz (55g) butter, softened
4oz (115g) plain flour
2oz (55g) sugar (for the topping)
A pinch of salt
Custard (optional)

1 Begin by gathering the yummy fruits that will make the filling for your crumble. Cooking apples are a great base (non-cooking varieties will also work), and blackberries, rhubarb, blueberries and plums make lovely additions.

2 Peel away any skin then chop the fruit into bite-size chunks. Place in a pie dish and scatter over 2 tablespoons of sugar and the water. Cover with cling film and cook in the microwave for 4–6 minutes, until the fruit is soft. Allow the fruit to cool completely, then add more sugar if required.

3 Rub the butter and flour together with your fingertips until it resembles breadcrumbs. Stir in the sugar, add the salt and sprinkle over the fruit.

4 Bake in a preheated oven for 30 minutes at 375°F/190°C/ Gas Mark 5, until golden. Serve with a blob of custard and dig in!

1

2

3

4

1

2

3

4

Fruit roll-ups

These are a lipsmacking home-made version of a kids' favourite snack. This recipe is for strawberry and raspberry flavoured roll-ups, but you can experiment with any fruit you pick. They're a perfect snack to take with you on a picnic and are healthy too.

1 Pop your fruit into the blender and mix to make a purée. Add the honey and blitz. The mixture should be a runny consistency, so add water (a tablespoon at a time) if the mixture isn't pourable.

2 Line a baking tray with baking paper and pour the mixture onto the tray. Use a spatula to spread the mixture out evenly.

3 Bake in a preheated oven at 210°F/100°C/Gas Mark ¼ for 4–6 hours until the mixture is no longer sticky to the touch. If the edges start to burn, brush with a little water.

4 Peel the mixture off the baking paper and place onto a fresh piece. Use a sharp knife and ruler to cut the mixture into ¾in (2cm) wide strips.

5 Cut the baking paper into ¾in (2cm) strips, slightly longer than your fruit strips. Place the fruit strips onto the paper strips and roll them up into neat bundles. Tie together with string.

You will need
5½oz (150g) raspberries
1½oz (50g) strawberries
Blender
2 tbsp runny honey
Baking tray
Baking paper
Pastry brush (optional)
Spatula
Knife and ruler
String

86 Garden smoothie

Using produce from your garden to make smoothies teaches kids about the journey of food from garden to plate (or glass) and is a wonderful way to get them to eat foods they might normally turn their nose up at! Try out different varieties of smoothie based on what you have in the garden or can forage.

You will need
3oz (80g) spinach
Small courgette
Blender
Handful of sunflower seeds

Fruit juice, or coconut
water or yoghurt
Water

Chop the spinach and courgette into small chunks and pop into a blender along with the sunflower seeds. Add fruit juice and water to the mixture to the thickness of smoothie you prefer. If you like, you can use coconut water or yoghurt instead of fruit juice.

87 Fruity ice pops

On a warm summer's day there's nothing better than sitting in the sunshine with an ice pop that you have made yourself! Reusable ice-pop moulds can be purchased inexpensively online, but you could also use standard freezer pop bags. This recipe makes 16 ice pops in three flavours.

You will need
1 punnet raspberries
1 large orange, peeled
   and chopped
2 kiwis
1 lime
1 ripe mango
Blender
Honey to taste
Funnel
16 freezer pop bags or
   ice-pop moulds

To make these delicious ice pops all you need to do is put the fruits into a blender. We mixed raspberry with orange, kiwi with lime and kept the mango on its own, but you can have any flavours you like, depending on what is growing in your garden or what you have in the fruit bowl. Add honey to your preferred sweetness, then pour into the moulds with the help of a funnel. Pop in the freezer until solid.

Courgette, carrot and cheese muffins

These scrumptious muffins are full of garden vegetable treats that little ones will love.

1

2

3

88

1. Line the muffin tray with the cases. Coarsely grate the carrot and courgette.

2. Mix the self-raising flour, oil, milk, carrots, courgette and cheese into a bowl. Crack the egg into the mixture and stir well.

3. Divide the mixture into 12 muffin cases, filling them half full, and place on a muffin tray. Bake the muffins in a preheated oven at 350°F/180°C/Gas Mark 4 for 20 minutes or until golden brown on top.

You will need
Muffin cases
8oz (225g) self-raising flour
¼ cup olive oil
¾ cup semi-skimmed milk
1¾oz (50g) carrot
1¾oz (50g) courgette
2¾oz (75g) Cheddar cheese
  (grated)
1 egg
Makes 12

89 Hedgehog rolls

These little wholemeal rolls are the perfect accompaniment to a picnic. Kids will love getting their hands stuck into kneading the dough, and making the rolls into hedgehog shapes will make children much more likely to eat them! The rolls will stay fresh for two days in an airtight container.

You will need
9oz (250g) strong
    wholemeal flour
1 tsp salt
¼oz (7g) pack fast-action
    dried yeast
⅔ cup warm water
Raisins
Scissors
Skewer
Cling film
Makes 8

1. Sift the flour and salt into a bowl and add the yeast. Make a hole in the middle of the mixture and pour the warm water in. Mix to combine.

2. Pour the mixture onto a floured surface and knead to create a stretchy dough. Fold and push the dough for about 10 minutes.

3. Split the dough into eight equal-sized balls and mould each one into a teardrop shape. Place onto a baking tray lined with greased baking paper, making sure they are well spread out. Cover with cling film and leave in a warm place to double in size for about 30 minutes.

4. Remove the cling film and reshape the rolls into teardrops if they have risen out of shape. Use scissors to make snips to look like hedgehogs' spikes on the dough, a quarter of the way down from the pointed end.

5. Bake in a preheated oven at 400°F/200°C/Gas Mark 6 for 10–15 minutes until golden brown. You can test to see if the bread is cooked by tapping the bottom – it should sound hollow.

6. Move the rolls onto a wire cooling rack and leave to cool. Once cooled use a skewer to poke two holes for eyes. Push a raisin into each eyehole with a skewer or sharp knife.

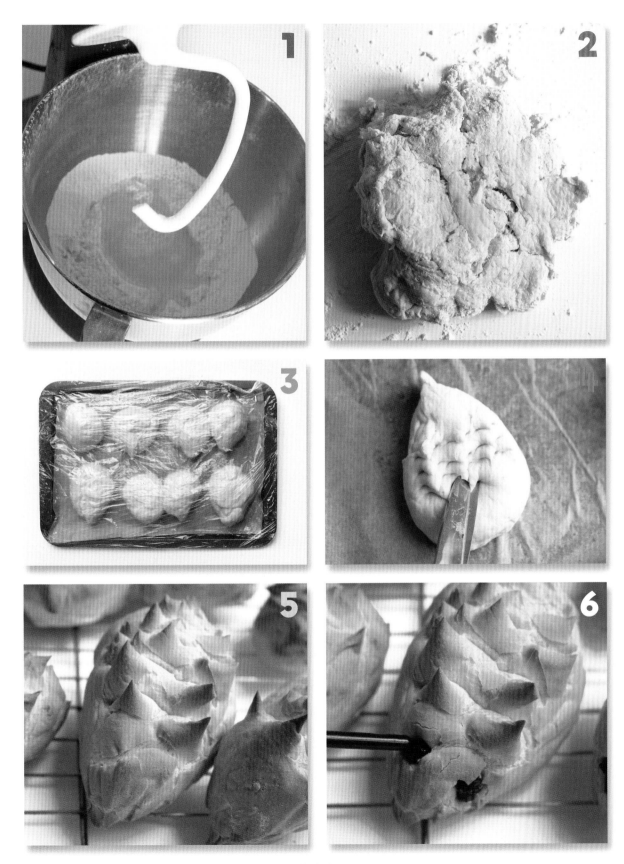

Playing and make-believe

90

Superhero mask and cuffs

Meet the newest superhero on the block – Captain Nature! The card mask and cuffs are decorated with flowers and leaves, so bear in mind they will wilt. If you want them to last longer, you can use pressed flowers instead (see page 89 for how to press flowers).

You will need

Pencil
Sharp scissors
2 sheets of A4 green card
Flowers, leaves and grasses

Craft glue
18in (50cm) thin elastic
Cardboard tubes
Double-sided tape

If you don't want to use flowers from the garden, grass and leaves work well too.

1. Use the template provided to draw and cut out a basic mask shape from green card. Mark two holes on either side of the mask for the elastic and poke through with scissors.

2. Head outdoors to collect a range of flowers, leaves and small twigs. Arrange them onto the mask so that as little card as possible is visible. Glue in place and leave to dry.

3. Thread the elastic through each side of the mask. Place on the head to fit, tie with a knot, and cut away the loose ends.

4. For the cuffs, cut the cardboard tubes in half, then cut them open along the length.

5. Cut the green card to fit around the tubes, leaving enough to wrap around the inside by about ⅜in (1cm). Glue the card to the tubes.

6. Cover the outside of the cuffs with double-sided tape, then attach the flowers and leaves onto the cuffs. Pop on your mask and cuffs, and you're ready to save the world, one flower at a time!

Mask template

Photocopy at 200%

91 Stick wands

Abracadabra! Sticks, pine cones and leaves can be transformed into easy-peasy magic wands in a flash. Go out for a walk to grab all the bits and pieces you might need in preparation for this project.

You will need
Glue gun/strong glue
Pine cones
Leaves or grass
Sticks (long enough to grip)
Yarn in a few colours

1 Glue a pine cone onto the end of the stick using a glue gun. Hold it in place until the glue has set. You can use painted pine cones – see page 74 to find a technique for this.

2 Glue leaves or grass onto the top of the stick, fanning them out around the pine cone.

3 Wrap yarn around the base of the pine cone and down the stick to cover the ends of the leaves. Secure with a dab of glue.

Fairy garden

This miniature fairy garden is a really enjoyable ongoing activity for children – why not add a few small, easy-to-manage plants that they can then look after too? Encourage kids to use their imagination and make the things that they want in the fairy garden using bits and pieces that they can easily find outside.

You will need
Handsaw/craft knife
Scrap of plywood (or craft foam)
Acrylic paint in yellow, black and pink
Paintbrushes
Twigs
Strong glue
String
About 50 lollipop sticks
Permanent marker pen
Pebbles, plants and grass seed

1 To make the fairy's door, cut a piece of plywood with a handsaw or craft knife to 5 x 2½in (12 x 6cm) – an adult should do this. Use craft foam if you cannot get hold of any plywood. Decorate it to look like a door – here it's painted yellow with a black window, hinges and pink frame. Remember to cover clothes and surfaces because acrylic paint won't wash out!

2 To make a swing, break four twigs to about 6in (15cm) and glue together in pairs to make upside down 'V' shapes with another 4in (10cm) twig between them to make the frame. Use five 2in (5cm) twigs glued together to make the seat, with string to tie onto each end and onto the top of the swing.

3 Make a little signpost by cutting a lollipop stick in half, with one end cut into a point. Write on your sign and glue onto a twig.

4 Now to set up the garden! Find a suitable location – on soil or grass against a tree or wall works best. Glue the door onto the tree or wall then stick lollipop sticks into the ground to create the garden fence. You can glue lollipop sticks across the fence to make it stronger and more realistic. Add a pebble pathway, a few small plants (sedum and thyme work well) and sprinkle with grass seed if needed. Add the swing, sign and any other items you think the fairies might enjoy!

93

Woodland animal masks

These fabulous felt masks are easy to make and are a good way to practise cutting skills. Use the template as a base to make your favourite woodland animals into a mask.

You will need
Paper and pencil
Scissors
Pins
Felt in a variety of colours
PVA glue and paintbrush
Large-eyed needle
18in (50cm) thin elastic per mask

1 Use the template on the page opposite as a base for creating your masks on paper – add ears, noses, beaks and any other basic shapes you like, as long as they can be cut from felt (so avoid patterns or intricate shapes). Cut out the templates, just along the outside edge for now. Pin them onto pieces of felt and cut out.

2 Use your drawing on the template to cut the remaining shapes out of other pieces of felt, such as the circular rings for the owl, the inner ear pieces and so on.

3 Layer the felt pieces and glue them together. Use a paintbrush to add the glue to the felt so that it does not go on too heavily. Leave to dry.

4 Use a needle to feed the elastic through each side of the mask, about ½in (1cm) from the edge of the fabric. Pull through and place on the head to fit, then tie the elastic and cut away the loose ends.

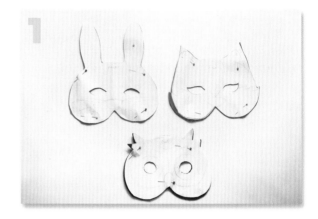

Mask template

Photocopy at 200%

94 # Feather headdress

This warrior-inspired headdress uses real feathers, which you can collect on a walk in preparation for making it. Save any leftover feathers for the dream catcher on page 83 and the bird's nest on page 20.

You will need
A4 red coloured card
About 10 feathers in
    varying sizes
Masking tape
Scraps of coloured card
    in yellow and black
Glue stick
Double-sided tape
Scissors

1 Cut a 2in (5cm) strip from the length of a piece of card. Draw and cut another strip, but this time add a 1in (3cm) triangle in the middle.

2 Glue feathers onto the back of the triangle. Secure the feathers with pieces of masking tape.

3 Cut up the scraps of card and glue them onto the front of the strip in a decorative pattern.

4 Use double-sided tape to stick the remaining strip of card around the back of the headdress to fit your head.

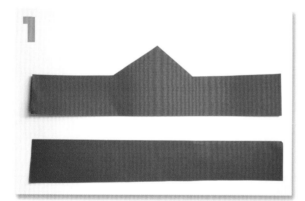

Stick people

You can make a whole group of these sweet little stick people. If you like, they can even be based on your family or friends! When collecting the twigs, try to find ones that have split branches so that it looks like they already have limbs.

1

1 Collect some twigs for the people, pine cones for heads, and moss and small fir branches for hair. Lay the pieces out flat and arrange them so that they each have two arms and legs, then glue firmly in place (an adult can assist by using a glue gun if that helps), along with a pine cone for the head. You can add masking tape to them while the glue dries to hold in place if needed.

2

2 Once dry, glue some googly eyes to the pine-cone head. Cut a length of felt to make a scarf. Snip the ends to create a fringe, then tie onto the neck.

3 Finally, glue a little fir branch or piece of moss onto the top of the head for hair. Then, if you like, you can think of other ways you could accessorize your stick people – have a look in the garden for branches and leaves that would make nice clothes, facial hair, handbags and so on.

3

You will need
Collection of twigs, pine cones, moss and small fir branches
Wood glue or glue gun (optional)
Masking tape
Googly eyes
Scraps of felt
Scissors

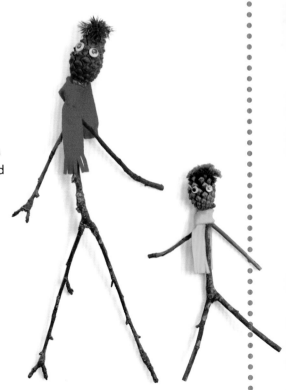

96

Toy's camping set

This little set is really easy to make and can be packed away when the sun stops shining – you could even take it with you if you go camping yourself. Try making a few in different sizes to get a real toy party started! The steps show a tepee for a 6in (15cm) toy, but you can adjust the sizes for a bigger one.

You will need

5 thick twigs (at least 17in/43cm long)
String
Waterproof fabric
Strong glue
Pegs
Scissors
Self-adhesive Velcro dots

Scraps of red and orange craft foam
A few small twigs
A4 piece of felt
Needle and thread
Child's toy, about 6in (15cm) in size

1 To make the tepee frame, take three of the thick twigs and push them into the ground to form a triangle, with each one about 12in (30cm) apart. They should be sturdy, so if they feel loose push them in a little more. Place the two remaining twigs in between the sticks, leaving a gap at the front for the opening. Tie the sticks together at the top with string.

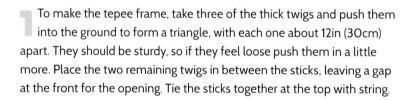

2 Fold the fabric over the tepee and trim at the bottom and top, so that it fits snugly round the frame, with the edges of the fabric out of sight at the back. Glue onto the sticks, using pegs to hold in place while the glue sets.

3 Cut down the centre of the fabric, on the front of the frame, to form a door. Attach Velcro dots to the flaps and side of the tent to allow you to open the tent. Cut another triangle of fabric large enough to fit inside the tent and pop it in to create a ground sheet.

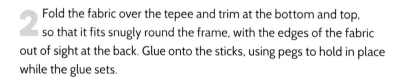

4 Make a fire by cutting scraps of red and orange craft foam into flame shapes. Glue them in between small twigs to create a pyramid shape.

5 For the sleeping bag, place your toy onto a piece of felt and draw an oval shape around it to create the base. Cut out, then cut another two-thirds of an oval for the top piece. Stitch together all the way round the edge of the felt.

97 Floral crown

This pretty crown features summer flowers including gypsophila and gerbera, but you could also use daisies, dandelions and leaves for a simpler alternative. The flower heads are wrapped in floristry wire in order to support and shape them.

You will need
Tape measure
Sharp scissors
Thin garden wire
Floristry tape
Fresh flowers and leaves (both with stems)
Floristry wire

If you want the crown to last, you could use artificial flowers instead.

1

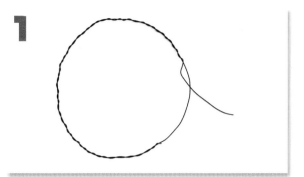

2

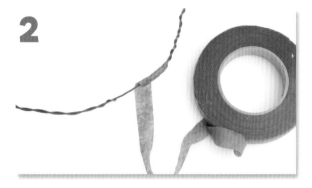

3

4

1 Begin by measuring your child's head. Cut a piece of garden wire that is double this length. Bend the wire into a circle the size of your child's head, then wrap the excess wire around it to create a sturdy band. Try on your child for size and adjust if you need to.

2 Wrap floristry tape all the way around the wire.

3 Cut the flowers so the stems are about 4in (10cm) long. Take a piece of floristry wire and wrap it downwards around the stem, starting at the base of the flower. Attach the flower by wrapping the wire around the stem and crown.

4 Wrap floristry tape around the crown to secure.

5 Repeat steps 3 and 4, adding on small clusters of flowers together. Wrap floristry tape around the clusters of flowers to conceal the ends of the wire. Keep filling up the crown with flowers and leaves in whatever design you like.

5

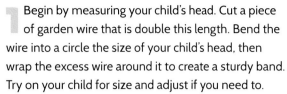

98 Wooden peg fairies

These little fairies make lovely additions to the fairy garden on page 129. Make them using leaves and flower petals as we have done here, or use scraps of felt or fabric for a more permanent finish.

You will need
Scissors
Yarn in different colours
Craft glue
Wooden clothes pegs
Colouring pens
Leaves, petals and small flowers

1 Make the hair by cutting around 10 strands of yarn that are about 6in (15cm) long for each doll. Glue the strands on top of the pegs, with the loose strands hanging down. Leave to dry.

2 Style the hair by trimming, plaiting or tying it with more strands of yarn. Draw little faces onto the peg dolls.

3 Now head outside to find suitable 'clothes' for your fairies. You could use petals, flowers, leaves of different shapes, feathers and so on. Arrange and glue onto your fairies, and leave to dry.

Woodland fairy wings

Sticky-back plastic makes these pretty fairy wings quite durable, and they are the perfect match with the stick wand on page 128. Pop the wings on and get ready for woodland adventures.

You will need
Coloured card, about 12 x 12in (30 x 30cm)
Scissors
5ft (1.5m) length of string
Sticky-back plastic
Leaves and petals
Glitter
Hole punch
String

1 Fold the card in half widthways and draw half a wing shape, filling as much of the card as possible. With the card still folded, cut the wings out. Cut out the middle as well to create a frame that is about 1½in (4cm) wide.

2 Cut a piece of sticky-back plastic that is slightly larger than the card wings. Peel off the backing and press the wings onto the plastic, sticky-side up.

3 Attach the leaves, petals and glitter inside the wings face down (as you are working from the back). Place another piece of sticky-back plastic on top to seal it all in.

4 Cut around the wings leaving about a ¼in (5mm) of plastic around the edge of the card to ensure the wings are sealed. Punch a hole in the middle at the top and bottom of the wings.

5 Tie string onto the wings to create two straps. Check and adjust the size before securing.

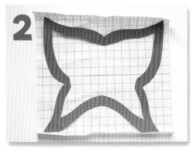

Musical twig instruments

Go on a walk and look out for good, sturdy Y-shaped branches in preparation for this project. Add bells and ribbon and you have a fantastic home-made shaker. You could make several with other objects, such as bottle caps, buttons or beads, to create different sounds.

You will need
Thin wire
Y-shaped branches
Strong glue
Bells in a variety of sizes
Thin ribbon in a variety
   of colours

1 Wrap the end of a piece of thin wire around one side of a Y-shaped branch, then add a dab of glue to secure it in place.

2 Thread bells onto the wire then wrap and secure it onto the other end of the branch with another dab of glue.

3 Tie lengths of ribbon onto the end of each branch and tie small bells onto the bottom of the ribbon.

4 Wrap ribbon several times around the main part of the branch for decoration, then secure with glue.

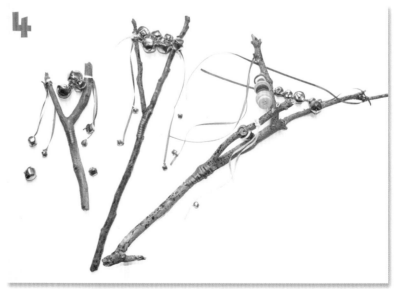

About us

We are Laura and Tia, two best friends, mothers, crafters and writers living in Brighton, UK. Both of us have been crafting ever since we were little and have happy memories of sticking toilet rolls together and making all sorts of masterpieces with our own parents. Now that we have little ones ourselves, we spend all of our time trying to think of new things to make with them. We began our blog, *Little Button Diaries*, as a way of documenting all the things we got up to. It quickly became an obsession and we love being able to dedicate time to making things for, and with, our children. We also wanted to show that, while becoming a mum takes over every spare second of your time, there is always room for crafting and a lot can be achieved, even if you only have a few twigs, a bucketful of pine cones and some PVA glue. We love getting outside with our children and we think it's so important for them to be out, even when it's raining or cold. It can take a bit of motivation (for us more than them!), but as long as they have the right clothes, kids can have fun in any weather. We hope you enjoy the projects in this book as much as we enjoyed making them and testing them out on our own Little Buttons.

Authors' acknowledgements

We'd like to thank our little nature explorers, Amelie, Harper, Lilah and Grayson, for always being eager to join in, for tolerating our constant photography and for testing out every single project in this book.

Index

To place an order, or to request a catalogue, contact:

GMC Publications Ltd

Castle Place, 166 High Street, Lewes,

East Sussex, BN7 1XU

United Kingdom

Tel: +44 (0)1273 488005

www.gmcbooks.com